Rhetoric of Everyday English Texts

£15.00

Rhetoric of Everyday English Texts

Michael P. Jordan

Queen's University, Canada
The Hatfield Polytechnic, England

London
GEORGE ALLEN & UNWIN
Boston   Sydney

George Allen & Unwin (Publishers) Ltd,
40 Museum Street, London WC1A 1LU, UK

George Allen & Unwin (Publishers) Ltd,
Park Lane, Hemel Hempstead, Herts HP2 4TE, UK

Allen & Unwin, Inc.,
9 Winchester Terrace, Winchester, Mass. 01890, USA

George Allen & Unwin Australia Pty Ltd,
8 Napier Street, North Sydney, NSW 2060, Australia

First published in 1984

Hum
PE
1408
J88
1984

British Library Cataloguing in Publication Data

Jordan, Michael P.
    The rhetoric of everyday English texts.
1. English language—Rhetoric
I. Title
808'.042   PE1408
ISBN 0-04-420047-1
ISBN 0-04-420048-X Pbk

Library of Congress Cataloging in Publication Data

Jordan, M. P. (Michael P.)
    The rhetoric of everyday English texts.
Includes indexes.
1. English language—Rhetoric.   2. Written communication.
I. Title.
PE1408.J88   1984   001.54'3   84-6183
ISBN 0-04-420047-1
ISBN 0-04-420048-X (pbk.)

Set in 10 on 11 point Times by Phoenix Photosetting, Chatham
and printed in Great Britain by Billing and Sons Ltd, London and Worcester

Contents

Preface	*page*	ix
List of Examples with Sources		xi

1 Introduction
Aims and Basis   1
Stylistic Analysis   2
Viewpoint of the Readers   3
Missing Information and the Integrity of the Writer   3
Selection and Presentation of the Examples   4
Learning through Analysis   4
Use of the Book and Indexes   6
Ideal Attitudes   7

2 Short Texts as Summaries
Writing as a Summary   8
Details Not Available   9
Relating Similar Items of Information   10
What Is Important Information?   12
Function as well as Description   14
Accounts of Problem-Solving Activities   14
The Metastructure 'Situation–Problem–Solution–
    Evaluation'   17

3 The Basic Metastructure of Information
The Basic Metastructure   20
The Family Doctor as a Problem-Solver   21
Conventional Order of the Metastructure   23
The Metastructure as the Basis for a Letter   24
A New Product as a Solution   26
Summary Aspects of a Short Report   27
Significance and Importance of Processes and Products   29
'Solutions' That Are Inadequate   31

4 Incomplete, Summary and Condensed Structures
Description with and without Situation and Problem   36
Descriptions of Historical Artefacts   38
'Solution' as a Complete Structure   40

'Solution–Evaluation' as a Complete Structure   41
The Common 'Problem–Solution' Structure   44
'Situation–Problem–Solution' Structures   47
'Problem–Solution–Evaluation' Structures   49
Introductory Summaries   51
Condensed Structures   53

5   The Signalling of Problems and Improvement
The Wide Scope of Problems and Solutions in Texts   57
Recognising Unsignalled Problems in Texts   57
Clear Signals of Problem   59
Deficiency with an Existing Solution   61
Improvement as a Solution to a Problem   63
Change in Situation or Circumstances   65
Improvement and Time Change   67
Problem Recognition as the Basis for Improvement   69

6   Recognising Different Problems in Texts
The Broad Scope of Problems   74
Decisions Signalled as Problems   74
Dilemmas and Decisions   76
Needs and Aims   77
Corporate Aims   79
Formal Requirements   80
Psychological Problems   83
'Need-To-Know' Problems   84

7   Evaluation Principles
Evaluation in General Terms   89
Two Parts of Evaluation – Assessment and Basis   90
The Combined Effect of Subjective Assessment and
   Objective Basis   92
The Significance of Figures and Units   93
Skilled Opinion and its Importance   95
Impartiality and the Need for Standards   96
The Essay: 'Situation–Evaluation'   98
Hypothetical Situations   100
Different Evaluations as Disagreements   101
Disagreement and Ruling   103
The Information Structure 'Situation'   104
'Situation' and its Evaluation   105

8   Evaluating Old and New Solutions
Pre-Evaluation of the Solution   110
Two Types of Evaluation of the Solution   111

Evaluation by Comparison 114
Recognising Problems and Proposed Solutions 116
Presenting a Counter-Evaluation 118
The Recognition of Deficiencies in New Solutions 119
Acceptance of a Deficiency in a Solution 121

9 Comparative Evaluation and Test Procedures
Evaluative Comments Preceding Revision 124
Asking for Constructive Criticism 125
Preliminary and Final Testing 126
Theoretical and Practical Evaluation 128
Comparison of Solutions (Value Judgement) 130
Testing as a Basis for Decision and Implementation 132

Appendix: A Guide to the Analysis of Texts 136

Indexes: A Information Structures 142
B Types of Problem 143
C Words of Coherence 145
D Signals of Logic 146
E Subordinators 147
F Hypotheticals 148
G Prefixes and Suffixes 149
H Time Indicators 150
I Informal Style Indications 151
J Key Words 152
K Subject Index 159

Preface

This introductory study is designed with many possible uses in mind. The obvious uses are as a text for 'communication' courses for students whose primary interest is not in language, and as an initial text for language students studying discourse structures and contextual grammar. The text is also suitable for use in advanced English as a Second Language courses and introductory courses in stylistics; with deeper analysis of the examples provided, the book could also be used in later years of language degree programmes. In addition, the book could be used in courses of journalism and in the education of teachers of English. Finally, it could prove useful for scholars of English usage and for researchers seeking to understand and test comprehension levels of sentences in context. Because of the wide range of potential users, few specialist language terms are used.

I am most grateful to Eugene Winter for his practical help at all stages of the production of this book. I am pleased to acknowledge that many of the principles of prose structure discussed here are based on his original research and pilot instructional manual *Fundamentals of Information Structure* (Hatfield, Herts: The Hatfield Polytechnic, 1976). Other colleagues at Hatfield Polytechnic have also provided useful comments while teaching some of this material, and searching questions from students at Hatfield and Kingston have been invaluable in helping me to form the final version.

I also extend my sincere appreciation to all the editors of journals and magazines who have given me permission to include examples from their publications in this book. Editors have been most helpful in allowing me complete freedom to do this, and I regret that I could not include examples from the work of all the editors who gave me this permission. Their genuine interest in the project has been a source of great encouragement to me.

Finally, I am pleased to record my gratitude to the British Science Research Council, The Hatfield Polytechnic and Queen's University, who helped financially with this work; to my wife Annie, who is perhaps beginning to tolerate the thousands of examples of writing littered around the house; and to my son Richard, who helped me with the compilation and checking of the indexes.

MPJ

Kingston, Canada
August 1981

List of Examples with Sources

Titles in square brackets have been made up to assist readers in identifying examples that have no specific title in the text.

1	Why Was the Law Changed?	Ontario Attorney General
2	HR 8752	International Astronomical Union
3	'Superplastic' Aluminium	*Engineers' Digest*
4	Liquid 'O' Rings	*Chartered Mechanical Engineer*
5	[Teething Troubles]	*Parents*
6	[Pioneering Polytechnic]	Made up
7	[Credit for Company]	Source not mentioned
8	Too Cuddly by Half	*Slimming Naturally*
9	A Growing Success	*Surveyor*
10	Sintered Carbide Improves Engine Efficiency	*Engineering Materials and Design*
11	Catastrophe	*Weekend*
12	Blow to Sex-Mad Coypus	*Weekend*
13	Short-Circuiting Telex Costs	*Now!*
14	Skirting with Disaster	*Practical Householder*
15	A Fresh Approach to Survival	*Professional Administrator*
16	Using Computers in Manufacturing	*Production Engineer*
17	Computer Seminar	*Production Engineer*
18	Not To Be Sniffed At	*Weekend*
19	VIVITAR Zoom	*Industrial and Commercial Photographer*
20	[Polish Lenses]	*Family Circle*
21	[Coffee Bean Ruse]	*Family Circle*
22	[Dear Parents]	Bayford Junior School
23	The Rhythm Method	*Living*
24	[Removing Stains]	*Family Circle*
25	Killer Blanket	*Safety*
26	[Plant Layoffs]	*The Economist*
27	[Alone!]	*Here's Health*
28	Tack Holder	*Practical Householder*
29	Keep Off the Wall	*Weekend*

30	Light Compressive Flange Loadings	*Engineering Materials and Design*
31	A Timely Test for Owen	*Titbits*
32	Alcohol Doctors	*Cosmopolitan*
33	Peening Process Prevents Intergranular Corrosion of Stainless Steels	*Engineers' Digest*
34	Depressed Mothers	*Cosmopolitan*
35	Membership	*Stimulus*
36	Alliance Prices Down	*Caterer and Hotelkeeper*
37	[Dull Teeth at Discotheque]	*Honey*
38	Closing Dates	*Chartered Mechanical Engineer*
39	'Clean' Electrical Power Systems	*Manufacturing Engineering and Management*
40	Pipe Bender	*Practical Householder*
41	On-Site Drilling	*The Plant Engineer*
42	[Changing the Colour of Hair]	*Slimming Naturally*
43	Improved Protection Pad	*Production and Industrial Equipment Digest*
44	Resealable Laminate Pouches Keep Moisture Out	*Production and Industrial Equipment Digest*
45	New Law in Louisiana for Married Couples	*Professional Administration*
46	Fire Resistant Ductape	*The Plant Engineer*
47	New Lens	*Safety*
48	Electric Motor	*Production and Industrial Equipment Digest*
49	Don't Be Suckers!	*Military Modelling*
50	Cup Crisis	*Family Circle*
51	Danger of Tyre Explosions	*Professional Administration*
52	Improvements	*Professional Administration*
53	Draught Excluder	*Practical Householder*
54	Pearlcorder SD Series	*Industrial and Commercial Photographer*
55	[Reduction in Spray]	*Sunday Telegraph*
56	A Moving Question	*Professional Administration*
57	OIL	*Now!*
58	Telephone Information Services	Post Office Telecommunications
59	Hydraulic Fluid Tests	*Safety*
60	How Can a Merchant Bank Help a Private Company?	*Professional Administration*
61	[Resin Products]	*Building Specification*
62	Stretch Marks	*Family Circle*

63 [Military Uniform]   *Military Modelling*
64 Love on Rebound   *Weekend*
65 The Right Handsets   Post Office
                                       Telecommunications
66 [Entrance Matting]   *Building Specification*
67 New Laws Aimed at Better
       Knowledge   *Safety*
68 Bridging Cavities   *Practical Householder*
69 Whistler's Mother's Cook
       Book   *Now!*
70 [Course Evaluations]   Queen's University, Canada
71 Vitamin Bee . . .   *Slimming Naturally*
72 [Report Headings]   *Annals of Applied Biology*
73 New Metal-Halide Lamp
       Features Long Life and
       Improved Colour Rendition   *Engineers' Digest*
74 [Evaluation of an Opera]   *Sunday Telegraph*
75 [Naphtha Consumers]   *Procurement Week!y*
76 Soaring Material Costs Lead   *Purchasing and Supply*
       to Higher Paint Prices   *Management*
77 Cameras in Court   *Professional Administration*
78 TV Commercials Need
       Watching   *Management Decisions*
79 [Dollar Strength and
       Inflation]   *The Economist*
80 Innovation   *Professional Administrator*
81 Too Lax?   *Here's Health*
82 The Hidden Ingredients in
       Bread   *Slimming Naturally*
83 Interest Rates: Gloom for
       Government   *Now!*
84 Fisher Dilemma on Fraud   *Sunday Telegraph*
85 6½ Prescriptions Each!   *Here's Health*
86 Working Alone . . .   *Practical Boat Owner*
87 [New Fused Socket]   *Production and Industrial*
                                        Equipment Digest
88 Reducing Finishing Costs by
       70%   *Automation*
89 [Committee Procedure]   Frontenac Court Committee,
                                        Kingston, Canada
90 Restrictive Trade Practices   *Professional Administration*
91 Future Work Concepts   *Original Equipment*
                                        Manufacturing and Design
92 [Timber Coating]   *Building Specification*
93 [Resisting Forces]   *Specification Associate*

 94   [Johnson's Shampoo]   *Cosmopolitan*
 95   Polyurethane for the Piste   *Design*
 96   Easier Rider   *Practical Householder*
 97   Teeth and Smiles   *Honey*
 98   Patients First   *Professional Administration*
 99   Your Chance to Speak   *Safety*
100   Chinese Pillpuzzle   *Cosmopolitan*
101   Bio-War in the Greenhouse   *New Scientist*
102   Improved Transmission for
         Cryogenic Power
         Transmission Cables   *Engineers' Digest*
103   CADC Helps Police with their
         Inquiries   *Computer Weekly*
104   Hats Save Heat   *Family Circle*
105   Biofeedback Stops Reynaud's
         Attack   *Here's Health*
106   'Hazfile' Computer Launch   *Safety*

This book is respectfully dedicated to those linguists who have kept their heads on the surface while all about them have been losing theirs in the deep.

Chapter 1

Introduction

Aims and Basis

The main aim of this book is to enable you to explore and understand structures in everyday English prose and the features of language that signal those structures. Selected short texts of well-written prose are presented and analysed within a consistent theoretical framework. After you have worked through the texts and the analyses provided, you will be able to see for yourself that they demonstrate and represent a commonly held unconscious consensus as to what constitutes acceptable written English. You will also see that each text is a model of a certain structure that is common in everyday written English.

The overall framework of discussion encompasses four main types of information (Situation–Problem–Solution–Evaluation) and many related subtypes of information – an approach which is consistent with the structure for analysis of plays and novels (Setting and Exposition–Complication–Resolution–Dénouement). In total, the discussion, the texts and their analysis offer a readily comprehensible basis for the critical assessment of texts in formal lectures or classroom discussion. They provide the means by which you can discern and judge the merits and demerits of written English texts in practical criticism.

Besides learning about prose structures and their signalling through use of this book, you can also develop a sense of style, and an understanding of grammatical and word choices and the adequacy of communications written for specific purposes. In addition to studying the prose structures explained in the analyses, examine the titles, the paragraphing, the sentence patterns, the length and complexity of sentences, the word choice and the punctuation of the texts. The analysis given with each text cannot possibly draw your attention to all possible interesting features of each text – you must learn to notice and appreciate them for yourself. However, some points of particular interest relating to the sentence structure, grammar, word choice, or rhetorical technique are briefly noted in the analyses. If you study all the examples in this book carefully and understand the structures contained within them and the words that signal these structures, you will have learned a great deal about the use of English. If you can also learn from the grammar, sentence structure, word choice and rhetoric, you will gain a deeper grasp of English.

Stylistic Analysis

Although the main purpose of this book is to introduce you to the fundamentals of English prose structures, the diversity of texts presented here provides an opportunity for you to study style as well. Some brief comments on stylistic guidance are given where texts are of specific stylistic interest, and these comments are consistent with the approach taken in *Investigating English Style* by D. Crystal and D. Davy (London: Longman, 1969). Their book contains analyses of conversation, commentary, the language of religion, newspaper reporting and legal documents. The texts I have included here were written as news or entertainment for the general public, for technical or business communication purposes, for 'soft-sell' promotion of products or services, as 'hard-sell' advertisements, or as letters requesting or giving information. This selection complements Crystal and Davy's texts.

Obvious stylistic features can be seen in advertisements. Note the contractions, use of questions, short sentences and paragraphs, and the use of *we* and *you* in Example 60. At the other stylistic extreme, Example 61 has a more formal style in which these stylistic features are absent and the use of the passive is significant. Between these extremes are the general interest texts (e.g. Example 64) which have some of the features of advertising style – short sentences and paragraphs, for instance. These basic stylistic features are readily observed, but a thorough analysis of style must also include a study of the grammar, sentence patterns and word choices. *English in Advertising* by G. Leech (London: Longman, 1966) is recommended for those interested in further study of advertisements.

You can only fully appreciate the structure and style of a text when you understand the purpose of that type (or 'genre') of text. The purpose of advertisements, for example, is to interest, promote and sell, and both the information presented and the manner of its presentation reflect this purpose. The analysis must take this into account. A comparison of advertising and formal technical writing is revealing. For advertising, the basis for a statement is often a vague opinion; for technical texts, the basis is usually more specific – often as actual measured data. One reason for including technical texts in this book is that they are generally more specific of detail than texts in other genres.

Viewpoint of the Readers

Texts are written not just for specific purposes, but also for specific readers, and this again is reflected in the information presented and the way it is presented. A text explaining a change in the law written for the general public (Example 1) will be different in content and style from a text explaining a change in the law to a professional audience (Example 45). Because the two groups of readers have different interests, specialist knowledge and related vocabulary, we must expect corresponding differences in all aspects of the text.

You need to learn many of the principles of prose structure from examples you can follow easily so that you can understand the informational needs of readers. However, you also need to analyse more difficult examples for which you must rely much more on your developing knowledge of language structures and signals. Only then will you fully appreciate the importance of writing that meets the needs of specific readers.

When you study Example 33, you may not know what 'peening' is, and the meaning of 'intergranular corrosion' may be obscure to you. You should recognise by the writing, though, that these and other terms will be known by intended readers. These readers will have some intuitive understanding of the structure of the text, but you will learn to develop an active detailed appreciation of the text which those readers will be unable to equal. You should have little difficulty in recognising, in the title, the situation (stainless steel), the problem (intergranular corrosion), the solution (peening process) and the evaluation (prevents). Other signals in that text will guide you to an understanding of its structure, even if you had no previous knowledge of the subject. You will find the analysis of some of these examples quite challenging, and very rewarding.

Missing Information and the Integrity of the Writer

A commonplace of good practical criticism is that a piece of writing is interesting just as much for what it does *not* say as for what it does say. The selection of material for a text reveals the intention of the writer and his estimate of the needs of the readers. It is often quite appropriate for writers to omit certain types of information when they are sure that readers already know it or can deduce it from other information given. Determination of what information is presented and what is *not* presented is given considerable prominence in the analyses.

One hallmark of a thoughtful writer is that he will tell his readers if some important information is not available to him (Example 3), or if he refrains from reaching firm conclusions until he has further evidence (paragraph 4 of Example 100; Example 90). He will deserve our respect even more if he perceives a possible misunderstanding on the part of readers and specifically corrects it (Example 92).

The viewpoint of the writer can affect the manner of presentation as well as the selection of material. In analysing a text, you must be aware that the writer may have some vested interest in presenting material in the best possible light. This is perfectly acceptable, but it does affect our analysis.

Selection and Presentation of the Examples

Examples selected for this book, in addition to exemplifying the usual standards of grammar, style, and so on, also present a sufficiently complete coherent account, containing enough information for us to examine the relevance of each part of the text. You will see from these texts that writers tell readers only what they want or need to know – and no more.

The examples are numbered consecutively and presented verbatim together with title, publication, date and other relevant information. To provide uniformity of presentation, the original typefaces and typestyles have not been followed; but the wording, paragraphing and any bold or capitalised type have been included faithfully. An additional general title is provided to summarise the main point of analysing that text, and where appropriate the paragraphs (and occasionally the sentences) are numbered to facilitate reference. In a few of the examples I have deleted information which you might have found completely obscure or which adds nothing to the educational value of the text; all such deletions are indicated by ellipsis points.

The analysis of each example is set in the same type as the example itself. The purpose of the analysis is to explain the main features of the structure of the text, and the principal words that indicate that structure. The signalling words are italicised. Because of space limitations, it is not possible to provide fully detailed analyses and you are encouraged to expand them yourself after a close study of the texts.

Learning through Analysis

In order for you to learn from the analysis of short texts, you will have to develop a keen awareness of the power of certain words that control and direct the structures of the texts. Within a defined situation, you will recognise a 'problem' in the widest sense of the word. You will become familiar with words that indicate this concept

– not just the word *problem* itself, but its near-synonyms *difficulty, dilemma, drawback, danger, snag, hazard*, and so on, and words such as *pest, unpleasant, disorganised, fear, smelly* and *illness*. Whenever we recognise such a word in the text, we expect the text to tell us of a solution (actual, attempted, or proposed), and solutions are recognised as things or actions that *avoid, counteract, reduce, prevent* or *overcome* the problem. Then the text may evaluate the effectiveness of the solution with such words as *excellent, important, quick, unique* and *failure*. Adverse evaluations are new problems, and again we would expect to be told of a new solution.

There are many complications to this basic pattern of Situation–Problem–Solution–Evaluation and these will be described in some detail. To illustrate the analytical approach used throughout the book, here is a text in which the problem is seen to be deficiencies in an old law. The example is part of a leaflet for the general public which we are told in the introduction 'briefly explains two important new Ontario laws which have changed the legal relationship of an owner or occupier of land and those who enter his land'. In explaining the need for The Occupier's Liability Act 1980 the pamphlet has to explain why the law was changed, and this involves identifying weaknesses in the old law.

Example 1   An Old Law Seen as Inadequate

Why Was the Law Changed?

The law was changed to solve two major problems. First, the judge-made common law, that previously governed liability, had become too complex to be understood by the public and was out of date. Second, the old law discouraged owners of rural land from permitting recreational activities because they feared being sued by permitted entrants who might injure themselves . . .

(*Property Protection and Outdoor Opportunities*, publicity pamphlet, Ontario Ministry of the Attorney General, 1980)

The question in the heading tells us that the writer has anticipated a question from readers and now intends to answer it, and we know that some inadequacy is about to be identified as there would otherwise be no point in changing the law. The defects in the old law are the stimulus for creating the new law. The first sentence tells us that the law was changed to *solve two major problems*, and this predicts that details of these problems will be given next. The first problem has two parts: that the old law was *too complex* (the word *too* in such contexts is a clear signal of problem), and that it is *out of date*. The second problem is the discouraging of a desirable permission for people to use land for recreation; and we can understand the reason for landowners not giving this permission from the last part of the sentence preceded by *because*, which signals reason. The reason is that they *fear being sued* if permitted entrants *injure themselves* (note the three separate problems here). Thus from this short text we can learn a great deal about the problems of landowners and land users, and the recognition of deficiencies in the old law as a reason for changing it.

In this example note also how the two problems are organised into two sentences and clearly signalled by *First* and *Second*, how the word *changed* in the heading and first sentence signifies the necessary difference between the old law and the new one, and that the style is quite formal and within the understanding of members of the public, the intended readership. Use of the compound word *judge-made* and the use of the question in the heading are both typical of advertising style, and these lower the formality of the communication and help to avoid general readers thinking that the tone is too official.

Use of the Book and Indexes

You will develop a critical awareness of English structures through analysis of all examples provided and through understanding the general discussion of the book. The discussion ties together the information gained from the examples into a larger body of understanding. Each example should be read at least twice before you read the analysis provided. Try to understand the structure of the text, following the normal sequence of the communication and recognising how the signals in the text tell you what type of information is being presented. Then read the analysis given and compare it with what you have observed yourself, remembering that the analyses are intended only to highlight main features. Finally, place the main features of understanding you have learned from that text within the larger framework of discussion for that chapter and the book, and continue.

Further texts are provided at the end of chapters, with only very brief guidance as to the main structures to be found in them. These can be used as the basis for classroom discussions or private study, and your analysis should follow the pattern established by the analyses in the book. In particular you should highlight actual structure signalling words in your analysis as these are evidence for the structures you are claiming for each text. You should work towards being able to analyse texts you find in magazines related to your own interests. Questions at the end of chapters are intended to remind you of the main points of structure and signalling found in each chapter, and these will prove useful for revision purposes.

Many useful concepts have been brought together in the indexes to help you to study parts of prose structures, coherence and style in greater detail than is supplied in the main body of the book. As an example, the concept of improvement is discussed in Chapter 5, but much deeper study is possible through comparative study of the texts listed under 'Comparatives' and 'Superlatives' in Index C. Finally, even further study is possible through the word index (Index J), where words such as *change, enhance* and *improve* occurring in the texts are listed and located so that they can be studied in their contexts. The many such possibilities presented by the indexes should be seen as a means of self-study by every reader of this book.

Ideal Attitudes

The best way to approach this exploratory study is with an open mind. You have probably received little instruction concerning the structures and signalling of examples of everyday English prose, and what you have learned about the genres of literary writing should not be applied blindly to the sorts of English analysed here. In any event, you can learn more from studying short texts of English for yourself than from hearing or reading about what some people think English texts should be.

Most of us have prejudices against one or more types of writing or speech in English, but these can only blind us to their structures and their merits. You may think that writing to entertain the public is childish and not worthy of serious study, or that technical writing is only for poorly educated technologists, or that advertising is beneath contempt. But these are all meaningful and very common forms of everyday English prose, and you are asked to put aside any such prejudices and to analyse and learn from their structures and styles.

The examples and analyses in this book provide the means for you to judge the effectiveness and veracity of the information, but first you should learn from the structures. Initially, take the information presented at face value, and do not waste time trying to catch the writer out on some point of detail. Once you have a sound grasp of the information as presented to readers, you will be able to make sound criticisms of the value and accuracy of the information presented.

Chapter 2

Short Texts as Summaries

Writing as a Summary

A writer only imperfectly perceives the part of the world he is describing, and he consciously selects the important information he feels best meets the needs and answers the questions of his readers. This 'window on the world' presented to the reader is thus an imperfect representation, which has to be interpreted by the reader in the light of his other knowledge of the world to create his own mental image of what is being described. This book is a study of selected examples of recently published short English texts which clearly exemplify the principles of structure found in all examples of such prose.

It is not possible or necessary for the writer to tell the reader everything (if he did, it would probably not be read anyway), so he selects the material he thinks the reader needs most (see Example 2). A writer often looks for information which he thinks should be there, only to find that it is not there. The absence of this information could be important, and it is often reported as not being there. If the writer thought that certain information might be available, then the reader might think so too, and the question that the writer answered for himself also has to be answered for the reader. Example 2 illustrates the selection of important information, and it contains information about the absence of something and also mentions information that has not been sought. It shows how the writer anticipates and meets the information needs of his readers, specifically answering two important questions the reader might ask. Even if you do not understand all the details of this text, you will still be able to follow the principles it illustrates.

Example 2   Negative Findings and a Question Left Unanswered

HR 8752

R. Barbier and J. P. Swings, Institut d'Astrophysique, Université de Liège, communicate: 'A well exposed blue spectrogram (dispersion 1.2×10^{-6}) of HR 8752 V509 Cas (IAUC 3382, 3390) was obtained on July 31 at the coudé focus of the Haute Provence 1.5-m reflector. No conspicuous emission is present, either at H_β or at other wavelengths. No search was made for filling in of absorption lines in this spectral region, which is known to be very crowded. A print and/or tracing of the plate is available on request for detailed study of our material.'

(Central Bureau for Astronomical Telegrams, International Astronomical Union, Circular 3399, 4 September 1979)

Only the first sentence of the quotation provides the basic important information, the remainder dealing with information not presented. The second sentence is a negative finding: they looked for emission but failed to find any. The third sentence answers the reader's question about filling in of absorption lines by saying that *No search was made* for it; thus the information is not available. The final sentence tells readers that a print of the spectrogram (plate) is available on request.

Note the changes in tense: the past (*was*) for what was done, and the present (*is*) for what is known to be true.

As with all brief reports and telegrams, Example 2 is clearly a summary of a much larger body of information. The purpose of the circular is to inform interested astronomers of a 'sighting' at a specified location and time, and the workers are offering their observed information to others who might wish to evaluate the significance of the spectrogram. The report is not intended to be complete in the sense of containing all possible information available, but it is certainly an adequate communication for its intended purpose. It gives readers enough information to allow them to decide whether they are interested in doing work on the sighting themselves, and it offers further information to those who are interested. The key to the success of the circular is in the appropriate selection of the information included, and the meeting of readers' information needs. Readers could well ask 'Was emission present at H_β or other wavelengths?', or 'Was any search made for filling in of absorption lines in this crowded spectral region?' The writer anticipates and clearly answers these questions.

Details Not Available

There are occasions when a writer does not know or understand all the information about a given topic, and his writing will usually reflect his imperfect state of knowledge. Where the writer does not have access to all the necessary information, his writing may lack vital details. Experienced writers learn to detect when important information is missing, and they will often tell readers that the information is not available to them, as in Example 3.

Example 3   Important Unknown Information Identified as Such

'Superplastic' Aluminium

1 Designated 'Superplastic Aluminium Alloy', a new material developed in Canada at the Alcan research centre in Kingston, Ontario, combines lightness, strength, and corrosion resistance with excellent formability. No details are given of the precise composition of this aluminium alloy, other than the statement that it contains zinc and calcium, but it is claimed to have properties which enable it to be formed readily into complex shapes by means of the thermoforming technique, in which compressed air forces the heated metal into or over moulds.

This is the first paragraph of a description of a new alloy. Details of the characteristics are given in general terms, but readers will want to know what the new alloy is composed of in greater detail than just that it is an aluminium alloy. They could well think that the lack of such detail is an important omission, so the writer has included the statement *No details are given of the precise composition . . .* followed by the information that it contains zinc and calcium – as well as aluminium, of course. The negation (*No details*) has significance as it indicates to us that the writer would expect that information. The *but* after the negated part mediates between what is not known and what is known by the writer. The final sentence is very long but presents no difficulty as it is clearly structured. Note the 'hypothetical' indication *it is claimed* in the final sentence conveying that the statement came from the manu-facturers and not the writer.

If the composition of the alloy had been no more important than its melting point or light reflectivity as items of information, then there would have been no need for the admission that such information is not available. It is because some information is more important than other information that meaningful selection is possible.

Relating Similar Items of Information

In Example 3 bundles of information are presented in related groups. For a chemical mixture such as a new aluminium alloy, we can visualise much of the information available as being in the form of a mountain, or an iceberg, with the most important features at the top as shown in Figure 1. The same principles apply to all descriptions; the actual contents will be different, of course, but the inclusion only of important information will always apply.

In this case the formability is so important that that characteristic is

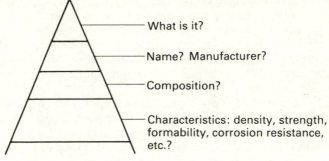

Figure 1   Details of description for Example 3.

incorporated into its name, '*Superplastic*', to stress that feature. Thus different parts of the information can be important and need to be stressed in the text. The description given so far provides a reasonable summary of the main features of the alloy, but other important questions have not been answered. These questions are 'What can it be used for?', 'What advantages has it over similar products?' and 'What problems can it overcome?'. There must be more information available, and yet this type of information does not seem to fit conveniently into the form shown in Figure 1. Answers to these three questions deal more with the function of the alloy (what it can do) than with its description (what it is). We can therefore identify two types of information, and these two types have been placed by the writer in separate paragraphs.

Example 3 (cont.)   Function Added to Description

2   Initially, the alloy will appear in three gauges, i.e. 1.6, 2.2, and 3.2 mm, and will permit the economical manufacture of complex parts too costly to make in aluminium by casting or stamping. Also, among other advantages, it can be TIG-, MIG-, and spot-welded or brazed without problems and can be preheated and painted by normal means and cured without a big loss of tensile strength. In addition, it can be anodised.
   (*Engineers' Digest*, October 1979, p. 7; summarised from *Iron Age*, 9 April 1979, p. 51)

Details of the expected use are given. This includes information about selected advantages (note the *among other advantages*) and information about its preheating, painting, curing and anodising qualities. The stress in this paragraph is on its uses rather than its description.
   The word *Initially* implies that other gauges will be made available later. The second sentence contains two ellipses in which first *it* (meaning the alloy) and then *it can be* are understood as part of the meanings of the clauses.

The text was a summary of another text from *Iron Age*; this in turn will be a summary from a press release from the manufacturing company. It does not affect our analysis at all whether the text we are analysing is the first version of a written text (a summary of the total information available) or a second or third version (a summary of a previous text). We shall see that the information structures are essentially the same.

The total information presented about the alloy can now be seen to be in two separate bundles of related information corresponding to the two paragraphs of the text. This information can be illustrated by two mountains of description and function as shown in Figure 2.

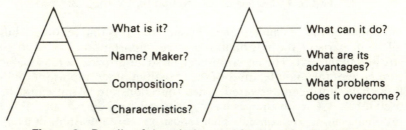

Figure 2   Details of description and function for Example 3.

Although this example is a technical one, we must recognise the general applicability of the discussion to texts describing events in all areas of life. What we learn from this and other texts must be generalised and not seen as applying only in this particular case or in one area of study. We will be studying texts from several fields, and it is not necessary for you to understand fully the technicalities involved to benefit from them. We are learning about structures and signals in English writing, and the specific information contained within the texts is largely immaterial for this purpose.

What Is Important Information?

Given that only selected parts of the total information will be included in a summarising report, we now have to identify the types of information that are most likely to be included. For this, we first need to distinguish between reports that simply describe something (like the first paragraph of Example 3) and reports that also tell us what it is used for, what it does, etc. (like all of Example 3).

In pure descriptions, where the purpose is simply to describe what something is, the writer has to select from a potentially very large (but finite) list of possible characteristics or attributes of the product or procedure he is describing. The description of every tangible thing can be broken down into attributes of that thing, and information is potentially available about each of those attributes. Every different type of thing has a unique set of attributes by which we identify it, and each thing of that type will have unique details available about those attributes.

For example, all electric kettles have a list of attributes that gives us a very good description of electric kettles generally. Such a list includes: size, shape, colour, weight, materials used, voltage, wattage, capacity, minimum capacity for use, overheating protection, and how it is held, filled and used. Different electric kettles will have different sizes, shapes, and so on, but they can all be described within the framework of such a list. Each item in the list can be seen to be a question which the writer must answer for his readers about the thing he is describing.

Thus each class of thing can be described in terms of its list of attributes about which information should be available, and each thing in each class can be described in terms of answers to questions raised by the attributes. Here are four lists of attributes about classes of things.

Parking ticket: amount of fine, where and when to pay it, offence alleged, authority issuing the ticket, what happens if you fail to pay.

Description of a person (for passport): place of birth, date of birth, sex, colour of eyes and hair, special peculiarities.

Form for a pedigree cat: breed, colour, breed number, pedigree number, sex, date of birth.

Dress: size, style and shape, material, colour(s), manufacturer.

The selection of material for inclusion in a description is manageable because we have a consensus regarding not only what information is potentially available, but also what items of information are more important. We know, for example, that the amount of the fine of a parking ticket is more important than the name of the person issuing the ticket; we know that the style of a dress is more important than the number of stitches in the hem; and we know that the breed of a cat is more important than the length of its whiskers.

In Index J many specific attributes are identified with the letter A, and each attribute is seen to be potentially the basis for saying how good or how bad (a problem) something is in respect of a certain attribute (e.g. efficiency). The attributes identified in that index are not specifically designed as a basis for checklists of typical types of information about specific things to be described, but they can be adapted for that purpose. As each type of thing has certain types of information potentially available about it, those engaged in analysing or writing about a certain class of thing can create their own checklist of typical types of information about their specific interests. This will provide a sound informational basis from which they can check or select information about a specific class of item, and choose the most important information from this list for each writing task they are faced with.

Function as well as Description

Each of the lists of attributes given earlier for parking tickets, and so on, represents elements of information which identify each of these classes on the assumption that its function is understood from the term used to name it. That is, if the title of a description tells us that what is being described is a thermometer, there is no point in providing the information that it is a device for measuring temperature. We all know what a thermometer is, and there is no need to include information that is known by our readers or is deemed obvious.

Everything being described can be assumed to be new to the reader in at least some respect; otherwise there would be no point in describing it. If the function of what is being described is new, then that becomes an important part of the description. If a writer is describing a specific parking ticket, he can assume that readers already know what parking tickets are, what they are used for, and so on, but the task would be significantly different for a description of a new 'smoking in forbidden area' ticket. For such a description, the purpose of the ticket, definition of the misdemeanour, when and where tickets are issued, the laws governing their use, fines imposed, and so on, would become essential information for readers. The description would adopt a totally different approach in that the purpose of the ticket and its function in implementing a given law would be of great interest to readers. The difference between a description of a parking ticket and a description of a 'smoking in forbidden area' ticket is an important distinction for this study. The former will only contain details of specific attributes of what is being described; the latter will also contain background information and details of advantages or function.

Accounts of Problem-Solving Activities

The types of information included in texts that describe function, purpose and effectiveness (as well as description) are to be found in accounts of problem-solving activities. Example 4 takes us through the main stages of such an activity, and from it we will be able to identify all the principal types of information available in texts. To help you follow this text here first is a summary. The summary has four clear parts to it (Situation–Problem–Solution–Evaluation) and these categories are expanded with greater detail in the full text, which follows it.

> During a recent routine test at Oldbury nuclear power station, a refuelling machine was found to be losing pressure and was taken out of service. The fault was traced to the failure of two in-accessible 'O' rings, and Flexane 60L was injected around them to provide a seal. On testing, the vessel was found to be completely sealed.

Now read the original report and its analysis, noting the structure and related signals. The sentences are numbered to help you follow the analysis.

Example 4   Complete Case Story

Liquid 'O' Rings

1   [1]The two charge machines at Oldbury nuclear power station, near Bristol, perform all the necessary handling functions associated with on-load reactor refuelling. [2]On a routine pressure test before a fuelling operation one of these machines was found to be losing pressure and it was therefore taken out of service and tested. [3]Ultra-sonic equipment was used to establish that the problem was in the lower flange of the main pressure vessel. [4]This is sealed with two 'O' rings, both of which had failed.
2   [5]A major problem arose because the whole of the vessel is encased in thick shielding; access to the flange could only be made through a special inspection plug. [6]Maintenance engineers decided to investigate the possibility of injecting some kind of plastic material into the inter-space between the 'O' rings and forcing it to spread out along the channel and seal it.
3   [7]The CEGB engineers contacted Sibex (Constructions) Ltd, a company which specialises in this type of repair work, and Sibex suggested Devcon Flexane, which they had used effectively before, as a suitable material. [8]Experimental 15 inch diameter flanges were set up to try the different types of Flexane and eventually a test run was completed successfully on a full sized flange using Flexane 60L. [9]This had the required chemical resistance and, in its initial liquid form, a viscosity of only 5000 centipoises, so it could be pumped successfully through the 1/8 inch diameter test tapping point which was the only available opening into the interspace – a cavity 0.008 inch (0.2 mm) wide by 14 ft (4.27 m) around the circumference of the vessel. [10]On curing, the Flexane assumed the physical characteristics of a resilient rubber.

4   [11]After the repair had been completed the vessel was pressure tested and found to be completely sealed.

(*Chartered Mechanical Engineer*, September 1978, p. 28)

The first sentence provides the situation, and we have some idea of the seriousness of the difficulties to come as we are told this is about a nuclear power station. The second sentence tells us of the problem identified during routine testing. One of the two charge machines was *losing pressure*, and the immediate solution was to take it out of service.

The location of the problem was determined after testing with ultrasonic equipment, and then the precise problem is identified (sentences 3 and 4).

The obvious solution was simply to fit new 'O' rings, but *A major problem arose* in the implementation of that solution (paragraph 2). The solution to the problem of inaccessibility was, in general terms, to use some sort of plastic sealant forced around the failed 'O' rings.

The third paragraph tells us how experts were called in to provide a specific solution, and they decided to use Flexane. They conducted tests first on 15 inch diameter flanges and then on full sized flanges and *eventually a test run was completed successfully*, the specific material used being Flexane 60L. The last two sentences of the third paragraph (sentences 9 and 10) provide evaluations of the chosen compound both in terms of its specific attributes and as a solution for this problem.

The final paragraph informs us of the implementation of the solution and the success of the final testing.

There are two instances of the use of the substitute word *This*, starting sentences 4 and 9. The referent (or antecedent) for the first of these is the whole of the phrase *the lower flange of the main pressure vessel*, and readers will know this because flanges are commonly sealed with 'O' rings and the main pressure vessel will have other sealing points besides just these two places. In contrast, *This* in sentence 9 refers only to *Flexane 60L* and not the whole of the phrase *a full sized flange using Flexane 60L*. Readers will know this from the technical content of sentence 9 – obviously a flange in liquid form would not be pumped through an ⅛ inch hole. You should thus see that the referent for *This* may have to be determined by the compatibility of the referent and the sentence of which *This* is a part. This rarely causes difficulties as long as readers have a sufficient general understanding of the subject being described.

Example 4 takes us through many stages of activity and related types of information. These are: the situation, the problem, the seriousness of the problem, the location of the problem, the specific cause of the problem, the reason why the obvious solution could not be carried out, the selection of a solution in general terms, the testing and selection of the specific material to be used, and the final implementation and testing. There are other types of information related to such a problem-solving procedure, but those included in this example provide an adequate starting point. All this information can be conveniently grouped under the four general headings Situation, Problem, Solution, Evaluation. Each of these groups can include a considerable amount of information and can include several subtypes of information.

The four-part structure 'Situation–Problem–Solution–Evaluation' is illustrated in Figure 3. This not only shows the four parts and typical subtypes of information associated with them, but also illustrates how the remaining chapters of this book have been structured around this metastructure of information.

The Metastructure 'Situation–Problem–Solution–Evaluation'

Example 4 includes more than simply situation, problem, solution and evaluation, and it should be clear that it still summarises a much larger pool of information about the series of events it depicts. It is an adequate summary of those events, providing enough detail to interest readers without going into the deeper technicalities that must be available on this subject. The level of complexity (and thus length) of the writing depends on the intended purpose of the report and the intended readers. The summary given earlier is a shorter account of the same series of events excluding some of the detail while still retaining the main elements of the story.

There is no question as to which version is 'better' than the other. The original text contains much more technical information and is more suitable for engineers eager to learn of a practical application for a product, whereas the summary contains very little detailed technical content and would be more suitable as an interesting item of news for readers generally interested in engineering applications. The summary has retained the elements of situation, problem, solution and evaluation; what have been lost are the specific details of the problem and of the testing procedure. The shorter the report becomes, the more of the 'other' types of information have to be deleted to make room for the essential elements of the story. The writer cannot stress details of Flexane 60L and leave out mention of the problem without losing the whole point of the account.

There are many variations possible around the theme of the basic metastructure 'Situation–Problem–Solution–Evaluation' and these are discussed in detail throughout the book and summarised in Index A. At the extreme we could imagine a title like 'Inaccessible "O" Rings Sealed with Flexane 60L' as a 'condensed' information structure including information related to the problem (the inaccessible

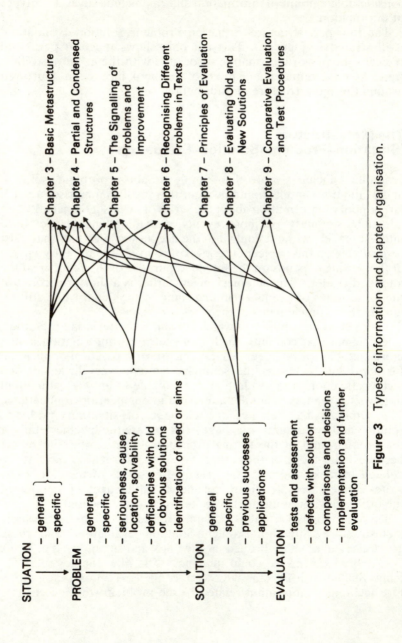

Figure 3 Types of information and chapter organisation.

'O' rings and their implied failure), the solution (Flexane 60L) and the evaluation (sealed), the situation not being included. The information may cease to be meaningful if the essential elements are not included in the text, and this book is a study of how this sort of information is organised and signalled to readers.

This book is not offering a simple foolproof method of analysis of texts which anyone can apply with little thought and trouble. Life and the language that depicts it are very complex, and an open-minded, flexible, sensible approach is called for. The basic patterns of prose structures are very simple, but the ways they are used and signalled by practised writers are varied and complex and we need to become attuned to these variations and complexities.

Chapter 3

The Basic Metastructure of Information

The Basic Metastructure

We have seen that the shorter a report, the more important it is to include answers to four basic questions:

'What is the situation?'
'What is the problem?'
'What is the solution?'
'How well did the solution overcome the problem?' (evaluation).

These questions are a valuable basis for anyone analysing or writing a report about a problem-solving series of events (and most are) or for anyone analysing or writing a creative story. Even essays of the 'A Day on the Beach' kind become more meaningful as an exercise when the writer learns to structure his story according to the necessary problems and solutions of any interesting account.

The meaning of 'problem' as signalled in texts is a very wide one and it is treated as such here. It means any form of dissatisfaction or other stimulus that makes us want to improve a situation. Thus within 'problem' we have to include an aim or ambition to do something, a short-lived desire, a decision or dilemma, a need or desire to create or improve something, a hazard or danger, an obstacle, a disease or discomfort, and so on. Types of problem are discussed in Chapter 6, and Indexes B and J provide a basis for further study of problem classification for those who are interested. This broad definition means that texts involving problems and problem-solving are extremely common in all walks of professional and personal life, and the examples in the book reflect this. It will be seen that the communication of problem recognition, solutions and their evaluation is an issue of central importance to all of us.

The basic metastructure can easily be recognised in the following report from an unspecified artillery post during the Normandy landings in 1944. '*Time*: 0628 hrs. *Type of Target*: Enemy Dispatch Rider. *Number of Rounds Fired*: Five. *Result*: Made Dispatch Rider Accelerate.' The unknown writer of that report had a sound understanding of how to communicate efficiently and effectively using the four types of information 'Situation–Problem–Solution–Evaluation'.

The Family Doctor as a Problem-Solver

A simple everyday occurrence will help to demonstrate how the metastructure of information is used in practice. A doctor in his surgery is faced with a situation: a patient comes into the surgery, the doctor looks at the medical history (including age, sex, previous illnesses and treatments) and weighs up the patient's present medical status (appearance, pallor, height/weight ratio, manner) in general terms. He thus has a reasonable basis for understanding the specific situation he is about to be faced with. The patient presumably has a problem, and the first job of the doctor is to try to discover in as much detail as possible exactly what the problem is.

As the patient may not know what the problem is but only what the symptoms are (e.g. bundles of pinpoint red rashes at certain parts of the upper body and arms accompanied by periodic sharp pains), the doctor has to determine for himself what the problem really is (probably shingles in this case). That is, he has to diagnose the cause of the discomfort experienced by the patient before he can hope to suggest an effective remedy. Occasionally, he may feel that the problem is not serious enough to worry about and he will simply reassure the patient, or he may need expert diagnosis to discover the specific problem. When he knows what the ailment is, he may suggest and/or provide a remedy which, when implemented, should result in the patient being cured.

In such a procedure it is possible to recognise four major parts of the thought–action process of the doctor and patient: determination of the situation, understanding and identification of the problem, proposing or prescribing a solution, and (after implementation) evaluation of the effectiveness of the solution by the doctor or patient. These four parts (situation, problem, solution, evaluation) are clearly identifiable highlights of the total information potentially available for any one series of problem-solving activities shared between the doctor and his patient. These four parts are well illustrated in the rather oversimplified story of Example 5, which is intended to represent a medical procedure

Example 5   Short Complete Medical Story

Jean: 'You look tired Sally.'
Sally: 'Yes, Peter's teething. I was up all night with him.'

Jean: 'You ought to try ANBESOL. Susie's teething doesn't give any
        trouble now.'
Sally: 'Jean was right. ANBESOL has soothed Peter's gums already.'
        (*Parents*, September 1979, p. 44; other details of the advertisement omitted.
        Original was in cartoon form.)

Sally, drawn and haggard, is at the clinic with her young son Peter, and
her friend Jean has recognised that she looks *tired*. The basic cause of
the problem (*Peter's teething*) and its serious effect (*I was up all night
with him*) come next, and this is followed by the suggested solution
(*You ought to try ANBESOL*) followed by the evaluation that it worked
for Jean's daughter's teeth. After the implied implementation of the
suggestion comes the evaluation that it indeed did work for Peter too.
The signals of time are worth noting in this example – especially *now*
and *already*; time indicators will be seen to be important structure
signals in many later examples too.

In this short story in very brief highlight form, we can recognise the
basic parts of the information presented, and from these we can
easily comprehend the total story being depicted. This is an example
of a very simple success story, where the situation quickly yields a
simple well-defined basic problem, which in turn produces a single
simple solution that works. Unfortunately life is not like that, and
both the thinking process and the writing that describes it often have
to be very much more complex. Here are just a few of the complications that can occur every day in dealing with medical problems.

(*a*)   The patient is new to the doctor, who may then have to find out
        the patient's general medical background before proceeding.
(*b*)   The doctor does not have the equipment or specialist skills to
        diagnose the problem, and he sends the patient to specialists for
        tests and diagnosis.
(*c*)   The problem is diagnosed but the doctor cannot treat the
        patient, who is sent to hospital for treatment.
(*d*)   There are several possible treatments (solutions or partial
        solutions), and the doctor has to evaluate the possible effective-
        ness and drawbacks of each before making a decision to suggest
        one treatment.
(*e*)   A solution previously prescribed has not had the desired effect
        or has serious side-effects, and an alternative must now be con-
        sidered.

These complications are only a few of those possible, and the number
of combinations of complications is very large and possibly infinite.
We cannot classify all the possible complications that occur in life and

that therefore also occur in writing, but we can recognise the basic structures and the typical complications that occur in texts. We are then able to apply this understanding to each new text we are faced with.

Conventional Order of the Metastructure

We usually describe events in the order in which they occur unless we have a special purpose in mind, and thus the conventional order of the four parts of the metastructure is 'Situation–Problem–Solution–Evaluation'. When a text is first written in this order and then re-arranged in a different order, it is usually quite easy for us to put it back in the right order. Try rearranging Example 6.

Example 6   Four Sentences Depicting the Metastructure

A   To remedy this deficiency, The Hatfield Polytechnic has pioneered work in the contextual grammar of English prose, in understanding how information is structured, and in applying this knowledge for practical benefit.

B   Professionals and teachers produce nothing except written communication, spoken communication and drawings.

C   This should lead to improved communications skills among students.

D   Yet in spite of this most students receive little or no instruction in the theory and use of information structures in practical communications.

There should be no difficulty in placing these sentences in the order BDAC, and it can be seen that the labels Situation, Problem, Solution and Evaluation apply to the four parts respectively. The correct version is:

> Professionals and teachers produce nothing except written communication, spoken communication and drawings. Yet in spite of this most students receive little or no instruction in the theory and use of information structures in practical communications. To remedy this deficiency, The Hatfield Polytechnic has pioneered work in the contextual grammar of English prose, in understanding how information is structured, and in applying this knowledge for practical benefit. This should lead to improved communication skills among students.

It is important to realise why this text as written can only be placed in this order for meaningful communication. The first set of reasons has to do with certain signals in the text that relate things in one sentence to things in another. For example, *Yet in spite of this* tells us that something in a previous sentence leads us to expect a conclusion and that this conclusion has not been drawn. In sentence A *To remedy this deficiency* identifies something in a previous sentence as a *deficiency* (a problem, of course) and indicates that something is now to be identified as a solution or proposed solution for that deficiency. Finally, in the last sentence something must have preceded it which *should lead to improved communications skills among students*. These are all instances of coherence between sentences. Two different types of the word *this* and words like *but* and *however* are included in Index C for students who wish to use the examples in this book for further study of this subject.

The second set of reasons for the order of the metastructure given is that it follows the natural time-sequence of Situation–Problem–Solution–Evaluation. Clear information-structuring involves both of these elements: appropriate selection of high-priority information with sensible ordering, and the effective use of signals in the text that tie it together into a coherent whole and help to guide the reader through it. Good selection of information and good arrangement of the material are not sufficient; structured writing also depends on the appropriate use of signals that tell the reader what type of information is being presented and how it relates to other items of information elsewhere in the text. We are here studying signals as well as structure.

The Metastructure as the Basis for a Letter

Writers often have to write a letter or report where they are required to complain about something or propose a solution to a problem. Such a letter can initially be structured in the form of the four-part metastructure and then filled in with whatever additional information may be necessary. Example 7 is a genuine letter written to overcome a problem. The original has been altered to avoid embarrassment.

Example 7   Simple Letter in Metastructure Terms

I was very pleased to see my article on 'Advertising Management Services' in the January issue of your Journal. However, you omitted to mention my affiliation with this company as their advertising manager, and this omission has caused me a little embarrassment here. Would it be possible for you to include this information as a simple 'correction' in the next issue? This would give this company credit for encouraging the use of the techniques I described and for allowing me to publish them.

The four sentences contain the situation, problem, solution and evaluation. The situation is clear in the first sentence, and then comes the problem with the change of type of information being signalled by *However*. The problem is in two parts: the *omission*, and the *embarrassment* it has caused. The suggested solution is given in the polite form of the question, and this solution is evaluated in the final sentence with mention of its beneficial effects.

In this example *This* refers to most of the preceding sentence, a fact we can see by substituting 'Your including this information as a simple "correction" in the next issue would give . . .'.

The basic metastructure only provides a brief skeleton around which more details can be built for longer reports and letters. Such a structure, though, could provide a sound start to the writing and in some cases it can be an adequate complete communication. The metastructure in practice ensures that the writing *feels* complete; such a simple letter will not give us all the detail, but it can be an adequate summary. Example 8 is also based on the simple metastructure. The use of the personal pronoun *I* in this and the previous example is worth noting.

Example 8   A More Complex Letter

Too Cuddly by Half

The letter in your June/July issue about how to keep your man in shape reminded me: Mine refused to admit he was gaining a spare tyre until, every time I got romantic and gazed lovingly into his eyes, I also knowingly grabbed a handful of spare flesh. This brought him down to earth with a bump and shamed him into eating more sensibly. Now not only is he slimmer and fitter, but there also seem to be more of those romantic moments.

(*Slimming Naturally*, October/November 1979, p. 13)

The first part of the first sentence (up to the colon) provides the situation of keeping men slim and the reason for writing this letter. The writer's problem was that her man was *gaining a spare tyre*, but the man did not share her assessment that it was a problem as signalled by *refused to admit*. Then comes her solution to complete the first sentence. The solution is then evaluated as shaming him into *eating more sensibly*, and this in turn results in the beneficial *slimmer and fitter* and the increased frequency of romantic moments.

The time signal *Now* is a clear indicator of the evaluation to come. The *not only . . . but also* contrasts the expected evaluation with the less-expected evaluation (the romantic moments). A more detailed analysis of this example is possible by considering things from the husband's point of view; such interactional analysis is beyond the scope of this book.

A New Product as a Solution

When something is being described for the first time, it is often very useful to describe it within the full metastructure of 'Situation–Problem–Solution–Evaluation' so that readers understand the background, significance and effectiveness of what is being described. The question as to when to use the full four-part structure and when to leave out some parts is dealt with in detail in the next chapter, but we first have to examine further examples of the full structure. In Example 9 there are five paragraphs and four main types of information corresponding to the four main parts of the metastructure; note the close correspondence between the types of information and the paragraphs. Uses of the dash in this example are interesting. The paragraphs are quite short and are typical of this sort of text, which is intended as a 'soft-sell' promotion of the product being described. There is another *not only . . . but also* structure in this example in which the writer put the appearance first as the more obvious need for the product.

Example 9   Complete Structure as a Clear Summary

A Growing Success

1 Apart from the readily acceptable advantages of traffic-free pedestrian areas, shopping precincts and the like, it is also nice to see that landscaping is playing an important role in the plans for most city centre developments.

2 A touch of greenery in the form of trees and shrubs does wonders for the environment but retaining its growth can sometimes be a problem.

3 Amazingly enough it is industrial designers who are helping to overcome some of these problems with such ideas as the Precinct Tree Grid – a Brickhouse Dudley product which has received an award from the Design Centre in London.

4 The Precinct was designed not only to enhance the appearance of trees sited in pedestrian areas – but also to improve their irrigation with an attractively shaped grid which allows the all-important rainwater to reach the tree's roots.

5 Manufactured in cast iron, the Precinct is available in three shapes – square, six-sided, or twelve-sided – and it comes in either 1160mm or 1200mm sizes with either a 450mm or 500mm aperture.

(*Surveyor*, 26 April 1979, p. 2 of insert; a photograph accompanied this text)

The first paragraph provides the situation within which the 'Precinct Tree Grid' is to be described. The situation provides the background by stating that it is nice to see landscaping *playing an important role in the plans for most city centre developments*. This is the framework within which we will understand the significance of what is about to be described. The *also nice* evaluates both parts of the sentence.

The advantageous effect (*does wonders*) of *A touch of greenery* is mentioned, but then (signalled by *but*) we have a *problem* with achieving a touch of greenery.

Then comes the solution to the problem, the *Precinct Tree Grid*, together with some details of its designers, its manufacturers and the receipt of an award. Note how the words *helping to overcome some of these problems* pre-evaluate the new product as being an adequate partial solution to the problem.

The fourth paragraph evaluates the advantages of the Precinct Tree Grid: not only enhancing the appearance of trees, but also improving their irrigation. It is the improvement in irrigation that solves the stated problem of growth retention. The final paragraph provides further detail about other attributes of the new product.

Summary Aspects of a Short Report

The summary aspects of Example 9 are very interesting. The first paragraph provides us with a general picture of a very complex situation, and we recognise that there are thousands of city centres for which this discussion is applicable. The text represents all such specific situations in a general way and thus provides a general picture within which we understand the value of the product to be described. The general situation for discussion is city centre developments, and specific situations within this are identified (*traffic-free pedestrian areas, shopping precincts, and the like*). Landscaping is identified as the situation to be discussed in further detail (see Figure 4).

Similarly, although only one problem is specifically mentioned (retaining the growth of the greenery), there are other implied problems associated with the general appearance of the city centre developments. The existence of these other problems is made clear by *some of these problems* in the third paragraph, which tells us that the solution to the stated problem must also overcome other problems too – one of which (the need for it to be attractive in appearance) is later identified.

There are also many solutions to these problems, as we can see from the use of *such ideas as*. Each of these solutions will meet the problems to a greater or lesser extent compared with the solution described, and there will therefore be evaluations of these other

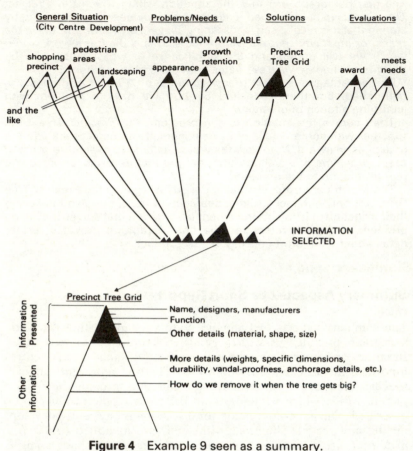

Figure 4   Example 9 seen as a summary.

solutions available in the total information about this subject. As this
particular solution has won an award, we also know that there has
been some comparative value judgement made in which this product
has been compared with others.

In selecting the material for inclusion in this text, the writer has
decided to concentrate on one main problem with mention of others
(particularly appearance), and he has also chosen to describe just one
solution to this problem while mentioning in passing that there are
others available. The text is thus a summary of a very complex set of
information available to the writer in this case about encouraging the
growth of greenery in city centre developments; the reader can gain
a glimpse of this total complexity while still learning about the
information that the writer has decided to concentrate on. His reason

for concentrating on the Precinct Tree Grid, of course, was to bring its virtues to the attention of readers.

Now let us examine the order of the information in the text and how selection of one type of information affects the information to follow. Within the broad situation of city centre development, the writer selects landscaping as the more specific situation to be dealt with. This decision then restricts and controls the direction of the details to follow. That is, the introductory information limits and guides the type of information that follows. Within the landscaping situation, the writer then further restricts the discussion through mention of the problem of growth retention that had to be solved, and the writing is restricted still more when a single solution is introduced into the text. From this point, we expect to be given details of that solution in terms of how well it meets the main problem plus other details to give readers an overview picture of the solution. We are not disappointed.

Significance and Importance of Processes and Products

When a professional writer provides details of the situation within which something has been created, he is able to explain the significance and importance of what is being described. In Example 10 nearly half of the text is taken up with discussion of the situation so that the new material to be introduced can be seen as a solution to an important problem. The writer is promoting the new process, and he does this primarily by stressing its significance.

Example 10   Situation to Show Significance

Sintered Carbide Improves Engine Efficiency

1   The special properties of silicon carbide make it an ideal replacement for many metal alloys, especially those that have reached their temperature limits. Its use, for example, in turbine and diesel engines would allow the engines to run at increased operating temperatures which in turn would mean higher efficiency and lower fuel consumption. In the case of the turbine engine, if operating temperatures were raised from 1700 to 2500°F, efficiency would increase from 40 to 55 per cent and fuel consumption would be reduced by 25 per cent. However, until now, this development has been restricted due to the unavailability of a suitable sinterable material.

2   The announcement, therefore, by the Carborundum Company of the development of a new process for manufacturing sinterable silicon carbide powder which can be formed in commercial quantities into a variety of complex shapes is of particular interest to these industries.

3 The uniformity and fineness of the new powder produces sintered shapes with strengths of above 85000 lbf/in^2 at 2700°F. They have a theoretical density that is greater than 98 per cent, zero porosity and a surface finish that requires no finish grinding. For further details about this material, circle Reference No. 257.

(*Engineering Materials and Design*, August 1976, p. 16)

The first three sentences explain the advantages that would accrue if silicon carbide were used in place of many metal alloys operating near their temperature limits. The example of its possible use in turbine and diesel engines demonstrates, in general terms, how use of silicon carbide could *mean higher efficiency and lower fuel consumption*. This generality is made specific for turbine engines where the higher efficiency and improved fuel consumption are given specific values, thus demonstrating the extent of the possible saving. There is no problem until we come to the *However*, which warns us of the problem to come. The problem is then identified as being *the unavailability of a suitable sinterable material*. Thus the scene has been well set to show the significance of the new process. This is then introduced in the second paragraph as being a process that can manufacture the material needed for the high-temperature applications previously discussed. Details of certain attributes of the powder produced by the new process follow in the final paragraph, and this information can be seen to be the basis for evaluation of the powder. Finally, readers are invited to send for more information.

The words *for example, However,* and *therefore* are signals of the structure, and again a time signal (*until now*) is important.

The writer of Example 10 has selected the information he feels his readers will want to know most. His purpose is to interest readers in the new process and the new powder it produces, but he does not try to write 'eloquent prose'. He simply concentrates on what he thinks his readers may wish to know, hoping to hold their interest by explaining the significance of what he is describing. He does this by describing the background situation and then the problem that the new process and material now overcome. This is an important lesson.

The title of Example 10 is highly informative. It implies that there is a problem associated with *engine efficiency*, and that *sintered carbide* is a solution to that problem as it *improves* engine efficiency. The title is an effective 'condensed' structure within which are compressed situation, problem, solution and evaluation, and this brings out the significance of the silicon carbide at the start. Our attention is drawn not just to a new product, but more to what the material can do in terms of overcoming a deficiency. It is this that makes it clear where the interest of the readers lies. It is relevance to what the readers wish to know that matters, not merely the manner of description.

Note how the evaluations of higher efficiency and lower fuel consumption are given specific values in this technical example. This is an important feature of this genre which is lacking in consumer product advertising; see Example 94.

'Solutions' That Are Inadequate

In an ideal world, we would recognise a problem, find or create a solution, and this solution would immediately overcome the problem. As language must reflect the failures and disappointments of real life as well as its successes, we have to be able to analyse examples that describe inadequate solutions.

When an action is taken in an effort to overcome a problem and it is then seen to achieve that purpose, we recognise it as a 'solution' to the problem. However, when that action fails to solve the problem, it cannot strictly speaking be called a solution, and the term 'attempted solution' is better. The words *try* and *attempt* often imply failure (as in 'He *tried* to cook his own dinner . . .') and the term 'attempted solution' has this intimation too. When something is introduced in a text as a solution (as in Example 9), the writer is pre-evaluating what is to come *as* a solution; that is, he is indicating to readers that the problem actually has been solved, and that details of this solution will now follow. Pre-evaluations are discussed in greater detail in Chapter 8.

When an attempted solution fails to overcome the problem, we would expect there to be other efforts made to overcome the problem, and complex information structures can be envisaged; for example, 'Situation–Attempted Solution 1–Defects and Failure–Attempted Solution 2–Defects and Failure . . . Solution–Evaluation'. Because such a procedure can be quite lengthy and because failure itself can be an important fact worth reporting, we can also expect reports at various stages of failure, as shown in Example 11.

Note the informal style shown by the short paragraphs, the contractions, the extra heading, and the two uses of *But* as paragraph starters. Also note the puns *Cat*astrophe and *ratty*.

Example 11   Attempted Solution as a Failure Creating Another Problem

Catastrophe

1 If the men at the weather station on Marion Island are a bit ratty, it's understandable.

2 They're being overrun by cats that they originally brought in because they were overrun by rats.
3 The island, 1,500 miles south of Capetown, was rat-free until 1945 when South Africa landed a party of men to set up the station.

Easy

4 But some rats from the boat got ashore and bred to such an extent that by 1948 five cats were sent to the island.
5 But they ignored the rats and went for the rare birds which, having never been hunted before, were easy meat.
6 Now there are 3,500 wild cats eating 600,000 birds a year – and the rats are still around.

(*Weekend*, 2–8 April 1980, p. 120)

Dramatic effect is created in the first paragraph by giving the probable reaction of the weathermen first. The second paragraph summarises the problem (*overrun by cats*) caused by the attempted solution of the original problem (*overrun by rats*)!

The original situation is given in the third paragraph, and the original problem is given in the fourth paragraph (signalled by *But*). This is followed by an attempted solution (*five cats*).

The *But* of the fifth paragraph indicates the surprise of the failure, and this is followed by the newly-created problem of the birds being eaten.

The final paragraph tells us of the extent of the new problem at present (*Now*) and the continuation of the original one. The time signals *originally* and *Now* are important here.

Presumably a new 'attempted solution' will be devised to overcome both problems, and no doubt more of the saga will be told in due course. Example 12, again in informal style, shows how another solution is planned after one has just failed. Again, *now* is important; it indicates that, at the time of reporting, the decision to sterilise had been taken but not yet implemented

Example 12   New Attempted Solution Following Failure

Blow to Sex-Mad Coypus

1 The sex-mad male coypus of East Anglia are in for a shock. Scientists plan mass vasectomy operations in a bid to cut the massive rodent population.
2 The rat-like animals multiply like wildfire and maraud through eastern England, destroying crops and damaging drainage systems.
3 Trapping has failed. So now captured males will be sterilised.

(*Weekend*, 2–8 April 1980, p. 13)

The first two sentences summarise the report, including information on the coypus' possible reaction, the planned solution (*mass vasectomy*) and the aim/problem (*bid to cut the massive rodent population*).

The immediate problem of concern is the *destroying* and *damaging* stated in the second paragraph, and the rodents are seen to be the cause of this. Note that we are studying the meaning of words in context. Destroying crops is a problem, but destroying the rodents would be a solution.

The final paragraph tells of a failed attempted solution (*Trapping has failed*) and the new attempted solution of sterilising captured males.

The compound words *sex-mad* and *rat-like* are typical of this informative/entertainment genre, as is the climactic ending in the final sentence.

Examples 11 and 12 can be seen as progress reports in that they present information that is complete as far as the work has progressed at the time of writing, but the project has not yet been completed. A satisfactorily completed project means that the identified aim has been met or problem solved, and this in turn means that details of the evaluation (how good it is) of the solution should be available. Where work is incomplete or stops after a failure, we no longer have the full structure 'Situation–Problem–Solution–Evaluation'.

Questions
1   What is the significance of the four-part metastructure of information for analysing structured complete short reports and letters?
2   What is the meaning of 'problem' in its widest sense? Use your own examples. How does this affect our understanding of texts?
3   Why is the metastructure usually written in the order it is?
4   How can new products, processes and concepts be explained within the four-part metastructure, and what are the advantages of doing this?
5   How can writing be made interesting without the use of colourful language? Why is that so?
6   What is meant by 'failure' of a 'solution'? What action might we expect as a result of failure? How will texts reflect this?

Examples for Exercises
All the remaining chapters conclude with examples suitable for analysis after you complete the chapter. You should read the first two parts of the Appendix before attempting to analyse examples on your own.

13   *Short-Circuiting Telex Costs*   A basic structure with considerable detail of the cause of the problem. There is a time as well as a cost problem.
14   *Skirting with Disaster*   Details of the problem are defects with an old solution. Note the alternative given by the editor, and the related evaluation.

15 *A Fresh Approach to Survival*   This is taken from a large article, and information has been left out where indicated. The structure is exceptionally clear – note the effect of the headings. The fresh approach stems from a defined need and earlier failures.

Example 13

Short Circuiting Telex Costs

1 Microchips are helping American companies use telex more efficiently.
2 The technique is being pioneered by the First National Bank of Chicago, which sends 1,000 telex messages a day world-wide.
3 It discovered that each telex message costs about five dollars to send – and half the cost was accounted for by executive and secretarial time and other expenses involved in preparing the message for transmission.
4 Each message started with an executive giving dictation to a secretary. Then there was typing, checking, paper tape preparation, editing and transmission. So a typical message took about 24 hours to get through.
5 Now the bank has linked its telex machines to several electronic typewriters in each office – and so messages can be entered directly into the telex system.
6 The message takes 15 minutes to get through and administrative costs have been cut by 85 per cent.

(*Now!*, 8 February 1980, p. 29)

Example 14

Skirting with Disaster

1 I always seem to have trouble when painting skirting boards with either the carpet flapping back on to the wet paintwork or being left with a crease if folded back too firmly and held in place whilst the paint dries.
2 I now fold the carpet back, paint the skirting and then place scrap pieces of wood diagonally (at approx 30°) from floor to wall. The carpet happily leans against these until the paint has dried.
3 (Whilst correct practice is to remove carpets completely before decorating, we do accept that this is not always practical. – Ed.)

(*Practical Householder*, May 1980, p. 14)

Example 15

A Fresh Approach to Survival

1 There is no doubt that the Institute in Canada wishes to retain its link with ICSA world-wide but at the same time it wishes to achieve sufficient autonomy to be able to gain recognition as a Canadian professional body.

The Problem of Recognition

2 Recognition has been a problem for as long as most of us can remember. Lack of recognition is the prime cause of our decline in numbers; new students are not being attracted in sufficient volume to offset the natural attrition of members by death, resignation, retirement or transfer. It is hard to induce a person to become a student if we cannot show him that, at the end of the trail, graduation opens doors to career advancement.

3 Employers, generally speaking, fail to acknowledge our existence except as an off-shoot of an English body dealing mainly with people aspiring to corporate secretarial positions without being admitted to the bar. To counteract this, we need funds to mount a massive awareness campaign; but such funds can be generated only by gaining new fee-paying members! This chicken-and-egg syndrome has been with us a long time and every attempt to overcome it has been met with a singular lack of success . . .

A New Designation

4 Let us establish a truly Canadian designation, independent of but supplementary to the Institute's diploma, with wide appeal to a broad segment of administrators.

5 With more members attracted into our fold come more fees; with greater revenue come more services to members. From these flow the elements of more widespread recognition. Eventually, such a recognition could be enshrined in law as it is for engineers, lawyers and Chartered Accountants.

6 We speak of ourselves as professionals engaged in administration. Our new magazine is titled 'Professional Administrator'. It therefore seems logical to adopt something like 'P. Adm.' as our new supplementary designation – standing for 'Professional Administrator' . . .

Implementation

7 This solution to our perennial woes has the support of the Board of Directors; if it has the support also of members generally, we should move on it quickly and dramatically. Seed funds could be pried loose from the nest-egg which resulted from sale of our secretarial practice manual. A legal-orientation committee should be established immediately to determine whether we can follow this course with our existing charter or whether a new corporated vehicle must be created for the purpose. Thereafter we must address matters of standards, publicity and implementation.

(*Professional Administrator*, June 1980, pp. 2–3)

Chapter 4

Incomplete, Summary and Condensed Structures

Description with and without Situation and Problem

In Chapter 3 we examined texts describing how a product or process was seen as the solution to a specified problem, and there was some evaluation of the extent to which the solution overcame the problem. The significance and importance of what was being described was made clear through inclusion of the situation, problem and, where appropriate, some evaluative details. This is necessary whenever the details of the situation, problem and evaluation are not obvious or are not otherwise known by the readers. For descriptions where the situational details *are* known by readers, there will be no need to include that information, and we shall examine in this chapter when and how the full metastructure is reduced or condensed.

The difference in approach between inclusion of details of the metastructure and their omission is clearly seen in Examples 16 and 17, which describe almost identical events. The difference in descriptive approach is not due to any differences in the events being described, but to differences in knowledge of readers. Note the similarity of the structure of Example 16 to that of Example 6.

Example 16 Description with its Situation and Problem

Using Computers in Manufacturing

1 Whether you regard computers as a blessing or a curse, the fact is that we are all becoming more and more affected by them. Yet in spite of this, the general level of understanding of the power and weaknesses of computers among manufacturing managers is dangerously low.

2 In order to counteract this lack of knowledge, the Manufacturing Management Activity Group of the IProdE is organising a two-day seminar on 'Computers and Manufacturing Management' to be held at the Birmingham Metropole Hotel at the National Exhibition Centre from 21–22 March 1979.

3 The seminar has been specially designed by the IProdE for

managers concerned with manufacturing processes and not for computer experts. The idea is that delegates will be able to share the experiences of other computer users and learn of their successes and failures. The seminar will consist of plenary sessions followed by syndicates where delegates will be arranged into small discussion groups.
4 Further details will be published later.

(*Production Engineer*, November 1978, p. 4)

Here we have a structure of 'Situation–Problem–Solution', there being no evaluation as the solution (the course) has not been given yet. The first sentence describes the situation readers are faced with whether or not they like computers. The expectation from this is that readers should have at least some understanding of the power and weaknesses of computers. This expected conclusion is denied (signalled by *Yet in spite of this*), and the second sentence is seen as a problem – especially as the level of understanding of computers by manufacturing managers is *dangerously low*. The course is introduced as a partial solution to the problem by *In order to counteract this lack of knowledge*. The remainder of the example provides descriptive detail of the seminar.

As in Examples 6 and 7, *This* refers to most of the preceding sentence – the part after the comma. This can be determined by the test 'In spite of the fact that we are all becoming more and more affected by computers, the general level . . .'.

Example 17 Description with Implicit Situation and Problem

Computer Seminar

1 A two day seminar on effective use of computers in manufacturing management is being organised by the IProdE's manufacturing management activity group.
2 The seminar, to be held on 26/27 June at the Birmingham Metropole Hotel, National Exhibition Centre, will follow the Institution's policy of featuring speakers with practical experience who will be drawn from companies of widely varying size and products. Time will be made available for delegates to see the associated exhibition, which will include demonstrations of equipment.
3 Discussions will centre on four concurrent streams: The interrelation between design, production engineering and production control; Planning and control of material requirements; Planning of manufacturing resources to optimise capacity; and Control of manufacturing resources to optimise capacity.
4 Further details are now available from the Conference Secretary, Rochester House.

(*Production Engineer*, March 1979, p. 4)

In contrast with Example 16, this example does not mention the Situation–Problem background for the giving of the course. Instead it provides details of the course and allows readers to interpret the significance and importance of the course for themselves. The punctuation in the third paragraph is worth noting.

The writer had a choice in his description of the seminar: he could simply state the facts of the seminar itself and thus leave the Situation–Problem–Solution framework of the seminar for the reader to supply, or he could specifically structure the description so that the seminar clearly becomes a solution to an identified problem. Neither approach can be said to be 'right' or 'wrong'; they involve a choice of whether to make the Problem–Solution structure overt or to leave it to the knowledge of the reader. In general, we would use the first example when the seminar is first introduced as we would wish to show its need and the background; and we would use the second example when we assume that our readers understand that background and now only need to be told the facts of the seminar itself and not its need, purpose, and so on.

Anything that is created is created for a purpose, and it is thus created to fulfil a need or overcome a problem. Thus anything that has been created can be described within its situational background if desired and necessary, and the job of the writer can then be to explain the situation and the problem that has been solved. Description will still be a vital part of the text, of course, but it will become part of the discussion of the solution to the stated problem.

The difficulty of evaluating a proposed solution is made apparent by Example 17. We can provide some analysis of solutions even before they are implemented, and we often have to do that in order to decide which of several possible solutions to proceed with. However, the only really worthwhile evaluation of a solution comes after implementation when the writer can explain whether and to what extent it has worked in practice. Such matters are dealt with later. For now we can recognise the omission of evaluation of the seminars as being wise until the seminars have been given several times and some meaningful assessment of their effectiveness can be made.

Descriptions of Historical Artefacts

The situation and problem solved are of great importance in describing historical and archaeological artefacts. The historian or archaeologist is not just interested in the physical details of an artefact – he is much more interested in what it was used for. From this he can understand who used it and can obtain a glimpse of life in the society in which the artefact was used. From an understanding of the problems solved by several artefacts, he can reconstruct the life-style and habits of the society he is studying. Similarly, an antique article becomes much more interesting to the owner (and more valuable) when the function of the article can be explained. Example 18 shows how the interest of the article being described is made clear through the mention of the situation at the time of its use and the specific problem it was designed to overcome. The short paragraphs are an obvious indication of the informal style; the double meaning of the title is deliberate, of course.

Example 18   A Historical Artefact Made Interesting

Not To Be Sniffed At

1   Streets in the 18th century were so smelly that people carried perforated silver boxes containing tiny sponges soaked in vinegar, which they sniffed regularly.
2   The container was called a vinaigrette.
3   Sniffing the aromatic vinegar was also thought to ward off germs, and lectures on preventive medicine by Dr. William Henry helped boost sales of vinaigrettes.
4   The liquid became known as Dr. Henry's vinegar.
5   The boxes were in use from about 1700 to 1850 but, by the mid century, the vinegar was often replaced by smelling salts.
6   Early vinaigrettes had fairly plain cases with elaborately patterned grilles. Most were rectangular but there were circular, oval and many-sided shapes.
7   Examples with etched portraits of people such as Lord Nelson, or depicting well-known buildings such as Windsor Castle, can cost several hundred pounds.
8   But plainer ones start at about £30.

(*Weekend*, 2–8 April 1979, p. 9)

The first sentence provides, in brief summary form: details of the situation in which the vinaigrette was created; the specific problem it was intended to counter; and the use of the vinaigrette with implicit evaluation of its effectiveness.

The second paragraph gives us its name, and the third provides details of a second problem it was *thought to* counter: *ward off germs* (the germs being the problem and warding them off being the evaluation). We are told that Dr Henry used this second structure as the basis for his sales campaign. The remainder of the text provides details of the solution (the vinaigrette). In a more formal style, the final paragraph would have been included with the previous paragraph and preceded by a comma.

'Solution' as a Complete Structure

It is very rare indeed for a published detailed description to contain only details of what is being described without mention or even a hint of the problem it has overcome, the situational background that led to its creation, or some evaluative details. Such omissions are appropriate when the readers already know a great deal about similar products and can thus fill in the gaps for themselves (just as readers could fill in the details of the background of the seminar in Example 17) and we shall now examine such 'incomplete' structures.

In Example 19 the details offered will have little significance except for the intended readers. The writer is relying entirely on the readers' knowledge to place the new product in perspective with similar products. It is therefore rather technical.

Example 19   'Solution' as a Complete Structure

VIVITAR Zoom

VIVITAR have now made available their 80–200mm f/4 TX zoom lens, first announced at 'photokina'. The lens is offered from stock with the Minolta XG2 mount, and has an aperture range of f/4–f/22 and a minimum focusing distance from the film plane in normal mode of 1.9m (6.3ft). The lens is multicoated, has an accessory size of 55mm and features 'one touch' zoom and focus control.

(*Industrial and Commercial Photographer*, January 1979, p. 120)

Details of the new lens have previously been given as it was *first announced at 'photokina'*, and here selected important details are given to enable readers to decide for themselves whether it solves a particular problem or need they have. The details provided form the basis for the reader to make up his own mind, that is, to evaluate the product for himself.

Note the extended ellipses of subject (the lens = *it*) in the last two sentences for the coordinated verbs *has* and *features*.

In Example 19 it is not possible to evaluate the effectiveness of the new lens compared with others available without specialist knowledge of the subject. Discussion of the solution without other details (even the problem it solves) is only possible when the reader can place the information given within the total information available from his own knowledge of the subject. When this can be done, it is possible to have single-sentence structures that provide only a solution with the problem being clearly understood as the reason for doing what is suggested; this is shown in Example 20, which is very brief and uses the punchy imperative (*Polish*) for the solution.

Example 20   A Single-Sentence Solution to an Implicit Problem

17   Polish the lenses of your glasses or camera with newspaper – but remember to crumple it first, then smooth it out for polishing.

(*Family Circle*, April 1980, p. 29)

There are two situations here with a common problem that the glass becomes spotty or dirty and thus reduces light transmission. The text provides a solution to that problem by telling readers to use newspaper, and by telling them how to use it.

Many warnings provide only the solution, though some provide the problem and some give both problem and solution. A notice such as 'WARNING – Stand well clear of the ramps' on a large fork lift truck gives only the solution. The situation is clear from the position of the notice on the truck, and the problem is implicit in the possible danger from the ramps. As anyone standing well clear of the ramps is clearly out of danger, the effectiveness of the suggested solution is so self-evident that there is no need to evaluate it. 'Low bridge' and 'steep hill' signs are good examples of problem-only communications, and 'Mind the gap' has problem and solution.

All instructions and requests demand or ask for a solution, and the child's understandable question 'Why?' is his first move towards a knowledge of problem-solving structures in language. Surely, he reasons, there must be a reason for me to stop banging my brother over the head with a wooden skittle? That reason, of course, is the problem he is causing. To act immediately on an order, a soldier may have to learn to obey instructions without knowing why he is doing it, and military commands at the lower levels are often of this type: solution only. However, in more normal circumstances it is usual to ensure that people understand why they are being asked to do something, and that involves the four-part metastructure again.

'Solution–Evaluation' as a Complete Structure

In the examples in the previous section we either have to accept the implication that the solution will work or else make our own evaluation of the solution based on our knowledge of the subject. The writer does not offer any evaluation of the effectiveness of the solution described. We shall now look at some examples where the writer does include some evaluation of the solution. Example 21 is similar to Example 20 except that this time the writer offers some evaluation of the solution. It again uses the imperative for the solution; the contraction indicates informality.

Example 21   A Brief 'Solution–Evaluation' Structure

37   Pop a coffee bean under a very hot grill when you go into the kitchen to make instant coffee for your guests. The smell of the bean browning will make them think they're getting the real thing.

(Family Circle, April 1980, p. 30)

There is no explicit mention of the situation (guests at home expecting coffee) or the problem (not having high-quality ground coffee beans and the desire to make the guests believe we have). The two sentences provide details of a solution to the problem and an evaluation of the effectiveness respectively.

The writer has selected the colloquial *Pop* instead of the more formal *Place* to give an impression of light-heartedness and informality.

There is at least a hint of the problem in Example 21, but it is quite possible to have texts where the situation and problem are not mentioned at all even though understanding them is an important part of the message of the text. Example 22 illustrates how the reader's knowledge is an essential part of the message.

Example 22   Important Implicit Situation and Problem

Dear Parents,
The school is trying to ensure that all the children's clothing is labelled. To assist parents the school can supply IRON-ON NAME TAGS. The tags will withstand boiling, and are suitable for most garments. They can also be used to label gym shoes, satchels etc. They can be sewn on if required.

(Bayford JMI School, Herts, England, March 1980)

Without knowledge of the situation and problem for this example, you would wonder what the fuss is all about. However, readers will have that knowledge and will readily interpret the information given as being a solution to a very difficult problem. The situation is a junior school for children aged 5–11 years who wear a uniform. Problems arise when the children change for physical education, outside play or games because there are then many sets of clothes of the same sizes, colour and quality. Children do not always keep their own clothes neatly in one place, and there are constant arguments regarding which clothes belong to which children – hence the solution being adopted by the school. The tags offered to parents are evaluated in the last three sentences.

The effectiveness of texts such as Example 22 relies heavily on the readers knowing the situation to which the text refers and then recognising the problem and seeing that what is being described is a solution to that problem. That is, the situation and problem are not explicit in the text and can only be recognised through the reader's knowledge of the subject.

The last three sentences of Example 22 provide evaluation of the tags, but the evaluation discusses features of the tags and not whether the tags will overcome the problem. Thus we have to recognise two types of evaluation: whether or not a solution overcomes the problem, and evaluation of other features of the solution. These two types are discussed in greater detail in Chapter 8.

Example 23 provides both types of evaluation. Everyone reading the article from which this example was extracted will be familiar with the situation being referred to and the problem that needs to be overcome. The solution described and evaluated is, of course, just one of the many solutions available. The purpose of the entire series of three articles was to familiarise readers with all the solutions available together with their advantages and disadvantages (good and bad evaluations) so that the readers could decide which solution(s) to adopt for their own purposes. The use of questions, the dashes, the headings and the contractions are clues to the informal style. Note how the order good–bad places some emphasis on the bad points.

Example 23   Solution with Good and Bad Evaluation

The Rhythm Method

1 *How does it work?* Basically by trying to pinpoint your actual time of ovulation – the monthly release of an unfertilised egg – so you can avoid sexual intercourse during the time you're most likely to conceive. It involves charting your cycle for a period of about six months until you're totally familiar with it; taking and charting your temperature each day – there's a definite rise in body temperature just prior to ovulation – and watching for changes in your vaginal secretions as thicker cervical mucus is another indication that ovulation is taking place.
2 *Is it safe?* It's completely safe physically, but few women who use the rhythm method are ever free mentally from that monthly anxiety of possibly becoming pregnant.
3 *What happens when I want to try to have a baby?* You simply reverse the strategy and make love during ovulation. If your calculations are correct you should become pregnant quite quickly.
4 *How soon can I go back?* When your periods have returned to normal after the birth of your baby and you feel confident about working with your cycle again.
THE GOOD POINTS
5 The rhythm method is entirely natural. It doesn't interfere with your natural reproductive cycle or employ any mechanical device.

Provided you have an extremely reliable cycle and your calculations are totally accurate it will be 60 to 90 per cent effective as a method of birth control.

THE BAD POINTS

6 Unfortunately, for most women the rhythm method is a very, very unreliable method of contraception. Few women have a totally regular cycle – or a cycle which isn't affected by stress, illness or family upsets. All it takes is one 'freak' period to throw your calculations astray.

(*Living*, February 1980, p. 106)

The details of the method being described here are provided as answers to specific questions – a very clear and direct way of ensuring that readers have the most relevant information they are likely to require. Evaluations are given in the two clearly headed sections, THE GOOD POINTS and THE BAD POINTS, which provide good and bad evaluations of the solutions. Note that these evaluations are primarily concerned with how well the method overcomes the problem (i.e. how effective it is as a birth control method), this being the prime requirement of evaluations of solutions to problems. No mention is made, at any point in the series of three articles, of the general situation (people's need and desire to make love frequently) or of the problem (unwanted pregnancies) as these are clearly understood by readers and taken for granted

The use of the incomplete sentences in paragraphs 1 and 4 to answer the questions is typical of speech and some informal prose. The full answering questions would be 'It works basically by . . .' and 'You can go back (to using the method) when . . .'. The use of *you* and *your* signals informality and intimacy between writer and readers, and the use of *that* instead of *the* in paragraph 2 indicates shared knowledge and understanding.

The Common 'Problem–Solution' Structure

Where the situation is known by the reader or can be readily understood from the context of the information given, there may be little need to provide specific details about the situation involved. In addition, where the solution offered is presented as a solution to the identified problem, it may need no further evaluation. This means that there can be quite adequate short texts in which only the problem and the suggested solution to that problem are presented, as shown in Example 24. The crisp style with the imperative (*Rub away*) gives us the message in very few words.

Example 24   A Simple 'Problem–Solution' Structure

13 Coffee and tea can stain your china cups and mugs. Rub away the stains with salt on a cloth.

(*Family Circle*, April 1980, p. 29)

The situation is understood as being that of a household, and the problem is given in the first sentence with the word *stain*. The solution is given in the second sentence. The writer has not included a separate evaluation of the solution, giving the impression that it clearly overcomes the problem. The repetition of *stains* is necessary as *them* could refer to the cups and mugs.

Example 24 can be seen as a perfectly adequate communication which is complete enough for its purpose. A much more detailed text could be written by including details of the situation, extent and seriousness of the problem, possible alternative solutions with their different evaluations, further details of this recommended solution, tests describing how this solution works in practice, and so on. For much more complex and important problems than tea and coffee stains, such details become necessary. For the simple needs of this communication, however, the very simple 'Problem–Solution' information structure is adequate.

In Example 25 we can again recognise that much more information could be provided if the writer had wanted to. The style is quite formal.

Example 25   Problem with Remedial Action

Killer Blanket

Deaths among elderly people involving electric blankets have increased this Winter so a six-point safety check-list issued by the Minister of State for Prices and Consumer Protection last November is being published again.

(*Safety*, February 1979, p. 6)

The first part of the sentence represents a problem demanding a solution. The second part of the sentence tells us what remedial action has been taken (note the use of *so*). No evaluation of this attempted solution is given, and we are left wondering about the effectiveness of the action last November.

This text is easily recognised as representing only two peaks of the total information about the subject being discussed. We are told nothing about the situation, about the age and number of the victims, the circumstances of deaths, the common cause of deaths, the adequacy of the blankets, the adequacy of standards controlling the manufacture of the blankets, the effectiveness of operation and cleaning instructions, or the effectiveness of issuing the same checklist last year. It should thus be clear that a large report is possible about this subject, and that such a report would fill in the details of the situation, the problem, the solution and evaluation of the possible effectiveness of the solution. In fact a detailed list of contents could be compiled for a large report on this subject, based solely on our knowledge of prose structures which tells us what sort of information could be presented.

This is not meant as a criticism of the original text. It is adequate for its purpose, as it very briefly describes the problem and the remedial action taken without going into all the detail possible. Obviously the writer did not want to go into all the details for this report – he only wanted to familiarise readers with the essentials of the matter. These essentials are the problem and the action taken, and indeed this approach forms the basis for most good summaries: the summary presents only the peaks of information about the problem and solution, perhaps with a mention of the evaluation and situation.

Note how in Example 26 the order is reversed to create a simple 'Solution–Problem' structure. This is a brief news snippet intended only to inform readers of the outline of a larger story. The use of the incomplete sentence *Not enough orders* is an indication of informal style.

Example 26   Remedial Action and Reason

Vickers is laying off 350 workers at its Elswick defence systems plant. Not enough orders.

(*The Economist*, 29 March 1980, p. 85)

The problem *Not enough orders* is also the reason for the layoffs, creating a dual relation of reason and problem.

Problem–Solution structures are found frequently in advertising where the copywriter first identifies a problem or need which the reader might have, and then provides his solution to the problem, as in Example 27. The style of this example is typical of many advertisements with the heading giving the problem and the imperative being used for the solution. Note also the incompleteness of *Sincere, low fees* and *Countrywide Introductions* – a style typical of classified advertising.

Example 27   Problem–Solution in Advertising

ALONE! Meet new friends of the opposite sex. Sincere, low fees. Countrywide Introductions . . .

(*Here's Health*, January 1980, p. 131)

The advertisement is appealing to those who are *ALONE!* and this clearly is to be seen as a problem. The suggested solution is *Meet new friends of the opposite sex*, but the real message is that the solution can be achieved by using the service offered.

A new factor is introduced here: the basic problem is being *ALONE!* and the suggested solution is to *Meet new friends of the opposite sex*, this then being the problem for the next stage of action. That is, we decide *what* to do about a problem, but this leads to another problem: *how* to do it. It is to this second problem that the advertisement offers an answer. Readers will have to evaluate the possible effectiveness of this service for themselves, and they are given little information on which to base their assessment.

'Situation–Problem–Solution' Structures

On many occasions the writer does not need to mention the evaluation specifically as the reader will understand it from the context given. In such circumstances effective reports can be seen to follow the structure of 'Situation–Problem–Solution'. Example 28 is a brief letter written within this structure. The writer concentrates on brevity and clarity with the normal use of pronouns found in letters.

Example 28   A Letter with Situation, Problem and Solution

Tack Holder

Whilst making roller blinds, I had great difficulty in holding the tiny tacks that attach the blind to the roller. To hammer these tacks in was virtually impossible until I had the idea of holding them in the teeth of a small hair comb.

(*Practical Householder*, May 1980, p. 14)

The situation is made clear with the very brief and effective *Whilst making roller blinds*, which tells us what the writer was doing when the problem arose. His *great difficulty* is seen as the problem, and the result of this holding difficulty is the problem that the hammering in of the tacks was *virtually impossible*. The solution is to hold the tacks between the teeth of a comb; although this solution is said to be just an *idea*, we can assume from the word *until* that the idea was implemented and that it worked. Because this assumption is so clear, there is no need for a separate evaluation of the solution. The word *until* is very important as it tells us that the problem no longer exists. The infinitive group *To hammer these tacks in* is the subject of the final sentence.

The lack of a written evaluation of a solution is quite understandable when the solution is only a proposal. Although it is possible to evaluate proposals, it is not always possible to provide evaluations that are at all meaningful. We saw an illustration of this earlier in this chapter (Examples 16 and 17), when a proposed course about the use of computers in manufacturing was discussed in two ways. In neither version was there any evaluation, and it was pointed out there that this was wise because insufficient information was available for a meaningful assessment. The vaguer the proposal, the more difficult it is to provide an evaluation of it, and we shall be studying texts in Chapter 9 where the evaluation of a solution is made more specific as progressive tests on it determine whether or not it is a worthy solution to the problem (e.g. Example 102). Where, as in Example 29, the solution is no more than a suggestion or demand for action, then the lack of an evaluation is understandable. You should by now be able to identify the indications of the informal style for yourself. Note how *But* mediates between what can be seen and what cannot be seen.

Example 29   A Demand for Action as an Unevaluated Solution

Keep Off the Wall

1 The only man-made structure on earth that you can see from the moon is the 1,500-mile Great Wall of China.
2 But what you can't see from up there is the damage that has been done to it.
3 People have chipped off bits for souvenirs and stones have been used for building.
4 Now new laws are being demanded to protect the wall.

(Weekend, 2–8 April 1980, p. 28)

The situation is given in the first paragraph, and the problem comes in the second with the clear signal *damage.* The third paragraph tells us of the motivation that caused the problem, and the demand for action in the final paragraph is the solution being advocated. No evaluation of the demand is offered. Once more a time signal (*Now*) is dominant, and the *new* in *new laws* is a clear indication of a solution.

'Problem–Solution–Evaluation' Structures

For readers who are familiar with the situation within which something is being described, there is no need to state the situation. In the examples of the simple 'Problem–Solution' structure we saw how this worked, and it should be obvious that an evaluation of the solution could be added to the structure, as shown in Example 30. The style is formal and the bold type for the first four words is used instead of a title.

Example 30   Details and Evaluation of a Solution

1   Light compressive flange loadings have often been inadequately catered for by conventional gasket materials but this problem has now been claimed to have been solved with the introduction of Chilcott's Fibraseal.
2   Of cellulose and synthetic fibre composition bonded with nitrile (NBR) it has a compressibility of 34 per cent and a recovery of 46 per cent. Its high tensile strength and compressibility, low compression set, good recovery, excellent dimensional stability and long shelf life are some of its many advantages and it does not require special packaging or careful handling.
3   Applications for which Fibraseal is specially suitable are sump pans, valve covers, differential housings, machine covers, dust seals and for felt replacement.

(*Engineering Materials and Design*, August 1976, p. 41)

No mention of the general situation of the use and need for seals and gaskets is made as this is readily understood by readers. The problem is made clear in the first part of the sentence and we learn that something has been *inadequately* catered for, and it is actually called a *problem* in the same sentence. Chilcott's Fibraseal is *claimed* to *have . . . solved* the problem. Details of the product are provided in the second and third sentences, and we can see that some of these details are evaluative in that they tell us how effective the product is. The final paragraph gives us details of *applications* for which it is *suitable* – clearly an evaluation. The prime evaluation involves the words *claimed to have been solved* as the claim that a product solves the problem can be seen to be the main purpose of the product.

The conciseness of this example is largely due to the use of complex subjects associated with the topic of description (*Its high tensile strength . . . long shelf life* and then *Applications for which Fibraseal is specially suitable*), and also the verbless structure at the start of the second paragraph.

The role of 'Situation' is to provide enough background information for the intended readers to understand the problem being presented and to be able to place the information in the text in perspective with their other knowledge of related matters. Omission of essential situational material is perhaps the most serious error in prose by inexperienced writers. Details of situation should only be left out if the writer is sure that readers already know that information. Many students – through no fault of their own – become used to writing for teachers and fellow students, who know the background situation relating to their work. It then becomes very difficult to learn to include such essential information when readers do not know that background; this is why many students find an introduction so difficult to write.

The point has been made before that the simple structure 'Problem–Solution' is extremely useful as the basis for a summary of a larger text as it indicates the most important items of information. Example 31 illustrates the use of the 'Problem–Solution–Evaluation' structure as a summary, where the first sentence provides a clear idea of what the whole article is about.

Example 31   'Problem–Solution–Evaluation' as a Brief Introductory Summary

A Timely Test for Owen

1   Carpet salesman Owen Ryband found a way to beat the waiting list for a driving test.
2   While his mates were waiting up to 10 months, Owen cut his waiting time down to just four weeks – by taking his test in a 32-ton truck.
3   He waited two weeks to get on to a lorry driving course, then Owen, from Boston, Lincolnshire, spent another two weeks learning to drive a 'heavy'.
4   It cost him £390, but if he'd waited 10 months he would have spent that much on two driving lessons a week at £6 an hour.
5   And of course, a Class One Commercial Vehicle licence allows him to drive a car.

(*Titbits*, 12 January 1980, p. 33)

The first sentence tells us that there is an effective solution to a problem as Owen has *found a way to beat* something, and we know that what he has beaten must have been a problem. The fact that his action has beaten a problem is a positive evaluation of the effectiveness of the action. Thus there is a clear summary of the problem, the fact that there has been remedial action, and implicit evaluation that the action has been successful.

The second paragraph indicates the seriousness of the problem (the waiting for *up to 10 months*) together with the detailed evaluation as to the effectiveness of the solution: *cut his waiting time down to just four weeks – by taking his test in a 32-ton truck*. The third paragraph provides details as to how he did it, and the last two paragraphs provide further evaluation of the solution in terms of comparative cost and validity of his licence for normal cars. The final sentence is crucial as it shows how his plan allowed him to drive cars and thus overcome the problem.

Note the informal use of *mates* rather than the formal *colleagues*. The use of *And* to start a paragraph is only found in very informal prose as in this example and in many advertisements, and *of course* indicates that the writer expects many readers to know the information that follows already. The dash in paragraph 2 places emphasis on the final clause, which tells readers how he achieved his purpose. The title cleverly emphasises time as the main point of the article.

Structures of the type 'Situation–Evaluation' are dealt with separately in Chapter 7. These structures lie at the heart of debates, discussions and essays. The straightforward structure 'Situation' is also dealt with there. To conclude this chapter the use of introductory summaries is discussed further.

Introductory Summaries

Example 31 illustrated the use of introductory summaries. The most important parts of the total text are brought together in a very brief form, including a mention of the problem, the solution and evaluation that the action to be described is effective as a solution to the problem. Example 32 has three paragraphs: the first summarises the solution and the problem, the second tells us about the solution, and the third tells us about the problem. The style shows restrained informality, the made-up *anti-booze* being an interesting indicator of informal style.

Example 32   Summary of 'Solution–Problem'

Alcohol Doctors

1 An anti-booze doctor in every hospital is the latest attempt by French health authorities to combat alcoholism.
2 In a nationwide campaign, the French health minister said recently that plans were being made to ensure that over the next few years every hospital would have a 'doctor for alcohol', responsible for patients with alcohol problems – even if they were not admitted specifically for alcoholism.
3 France has the highest alcoholism rate in the world and alcohol is linked with some forty percent of road deaths in France.

(*Cosmopolitan*, January 1980, p. 23)

The first paragraph tells us of action (introducing *an anti-booze doctor*) which is seen as a solution now being implemented; there can thus be no evaluation of the action as yet. The action is stated as being to *combat alcoholism* and we thus see the action as an *attempt* at a partial solution. This initial sentence is a clear summary of the 'Solution–Problem' structure to follow. Note the parallelism between the informal *anti-booze* and formal *combat alcoholism*.

The second paragraph tells us that the attempted partial solution has been decided upon but has yet to be implemented – hence no evaluation – and the duties of the doctors are specified. The extent and seriousness of the problem are given in the final paragraph; these are evaluations of the problem.

Example 33 takes summary one stage further: the title summarises the text presented, which in turn we can understand as a summary of the total information available about this matter. This is how we have to understand summaries – as brief details of the important information contained in the body of the text. This two-stage selection of information is illustrated by Figure 5, to which is added a third possible stage where the title itself is a summary.

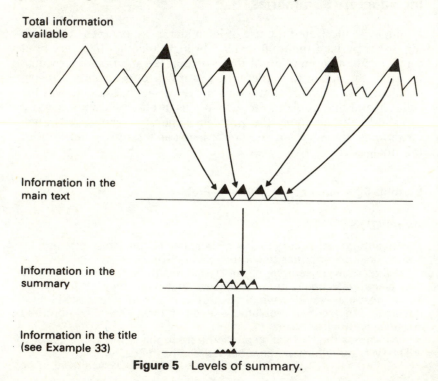

Total information
available

Information in the
main text

Information in the
summary

Information in the title
(see Example 33)

Figure 5   Levels of summary.

Condensed Structures

When there is quite a lot to say about the situation, problem, solution and evaluation, each part will have its own sentence(s) and often paragraphs. When the message is very brief, however, we often find that the types of information are condensed within one or two sentences. Introductory summaries can be of this type, and titles are even more likely to include different types of information in condensed form. The title in Example 33 is a good illustration. The situation is that of the making of *stainless steels*, the problem is *intergranular corrosion*, the solution is *peening process* and the evaluation is given by *prevents* which tells us that the solution overcomes the problem.

The details given in that title are not complete, of course, and they are not intended to be. The purpose is to give a very brief indication of the whole of the information structure to be included in the text. Titles can stress the problem, the situation, the solution, the evaluation, or any other information feature. They can also be very useful summaries of the information presented in the report.

A look at a few of the headings in examples we have analysed so far indicate some of the informational roles of titles. The title of Example 8 indicates a problem, clearly signalled by *Too*; the title of Example 9 is an evaluation of an unspecified problem and solution signalled by *Success*; and the title of Example 13 gives situation, problem and evaluation with details of the solution being left for the main text. Puns are very common in titles for less formal styles. Obvious examples we have already seen are 'A *Growing* Success', '*Cat*astrophe' and '*Skirting* with Disaster'.

Questions
1   Compare a description first with and then without information on the situation and the problem. What difference in knowledge of the reader would you assume?
2   What is the point of explaining the problems solved by historical and archaeological artefacts?
3   What are the two types of evaluation of a solution?
4   What are the differences between 'solution', 'attempted solution' and 'proposal' (or 'proposed solution')?
5   Why are so many advertisements so obviously involved with problems, their solutions and evaluation of the solutions?
6   What is the function of an introductory summary?

Examples for Exercises
Here are a few hints on how to go about analysing the examples that follow.

33   *Peening Process*   Three levels of summary; note the explanation of the increasingly severe aspects of the problem with logic signals of *thereby*, *As a result* and *causing*. Sentences are numbered to help with analysis and discussion.

34   *Depressed Mothers*   Problem, basis of problem and solution followed by evaluation. The adverse evaluation is a problem, so a suggested solution follows.

35   *Membership*   Implicit situation with two separate proposals to overcome the problem.

36   *Alliance Prices Down*   The problem (reason for the action) is sandwiched between details of the attempted solution.

37   *Dull Teeth*   Introductory summary followed by problem and solution.

Example 33

Peening Process Prevents Intergranular Corrosion of Stainless Steels

1   [1]It is well known that shot-peening can protect metals against stress corrosion cracking by producing a compressively stressed layer on the surface. [2]However, it now appears from the results of recent work carried out in the U.S.A. by the Metal Improvement Co. of Teaneck, N.J. that high-intensity peening of 300 Series austenitic stainless steels will also prevent intergranular corrosion cracking. [3]Apparently, when these Ni–Cr–Fe steels are sensitized by heating them to between 950 and 1500°F chromium carbides precipitate along continuous grain boundaries extending from deep in the metal to the surface, thereby depleting chromium carbide in layers next to the grain boundaries. [4]As a result, intergranular corrosion starts in the depleted surface areas and propagates down into the workpiece, causing failure of piping, pressure vessels, and other equipment containing corrosive fluids.

2   [5]The idea of the high-intensity peening process is to break up the grain boundaries at the surfaces by closely controlled repetitive cold-working of the surfaces by ultra-hard metal or ceramic shot prior to heat treatment or welding. [6]It is true that sensitizing temperatures will still cause carbides to form along grain boundaries below the surface of fillets or other workpiece sections, but carbides at the surface layer will be randomly dispersed and hence corrosive environments will not penetrate the surface. [7]At the same time, the peening process confers the usual protection against stress-corrosion cracking.

(*Engineers' Digest*, April 1976, p. 16; from *Design News*, January 1976, p. 12)

Example 34

Depressed Mothers

1   New fathers are ill-equipped to cope with the nurturing role says Vivienne Welburn in *Postnatal Depression*, out this month (Fontana, £1.25).

2   Of all the women Ms Welburn talked to who suffered from postnatal depression, only one had a husband who found help for her. 'Depression can be a slow quicksand, and a man preoccupied with his own problems can easily fail to notice.'

3   Men and their employers must be encouraged to take the home role as seriously as the work role, says the author (who suffered depression after her second child). One employer when discussing nursery provision for the children of female employees was astonished when confronted with the idea that fathers might also use the nursery. Statutory paternity leave and some leave for fathers when their children are sick might help to change attitudes, she suggests.

(*Cosmopolitan*, January 1980, p. 23)

Example 35

Membership

1   Concern over the lagging support of the general membership was the motivating force behind two papers tabled at the April meeting, both of which proposed remedial measures.

2   Gordon MacKay presented a Notice of Motion wherein he proposed that to qualify for membership in the Chapter a point system be instituted based on participation in Chapter and STC activities during the previous year. The notice is reproduced in this issue and will be debated and voted on at the first meeting of the next session (September 1980).

3   A second paper was the interim Report by the subcommittee on Feasible Methods to Revitalize the Eastern Ontario Chapter. Copies of the report may be obtained from the Secretary at the next business meeting in September. The Recommendations of the Interim Report are reproduced in this issue of Stimulus. Some of these will be incorporated in the 1980–81 season program.

(*Stimulus*, April 1980, p. 4)

Example 36

Alliance Prices Down

1   Prices are being cut on 50 catering non-food lines at 42 Alliance cash and carry outlets, and held down for a period of six months, from the end of March until the end of September.

2   This is an effort to build confidence and continuity in the catering market, Colin Avison, Alliance's managing director, told *Caterer* last week.

3   The promotion covers many disposable products, such as plastic cutlery, paper napkins, light and heavy duty dishcloths, dustbin liners, and stainless steel knives, forks and spoons.

(*Caterer and Hotelkeeper*, 6 April 1979, p. 14)

Example 37

Help is at hand for those whose dentures let them down at the discotheque. The problem is that while normal teeth fluoresce (that is they shine bright white in ultraviolet disco light) false teeth don't. Now a health care firm, Johnson and Johnson of New Brunswick, have patented false teeth that contain cerium and terbium salts which gleam as white as a newly-washed shirt front on the disco dance floor.

(*Honey*, March 1980, p. 12)

Chapter 5

The Signalling of Problems and Improvement

The Wide Scope of Problems and Solutions in Texts

It should be clear from the diverse subjects of the examples analysed so far that texts dealing with problems and solutions have a very wide scope. Now that you can recognise descriptions as being descriptions of solutions to definable problems, you should be able to see that many texts represent problem-solving activities. Because it is not always necessary to include all four parts of the metastructure, the structures of texts dealing with problems and their solutions and evaluations are very varied. In order to understand these structures, you need to learn to recognise problems when they are signalled in texts.

This chapter deals with general concepts of recognition of problems as depicted in texts, and the next chapter provides some discussion of the different types of problem that are communicated. The aim of these two chapters is to enable you to identify when the concept of 'problem' is signalled in texts and the sorts of signal in the language that indicate that a problem is, or was, present. Unfortunately (problem coming!), that is not always easy. Often there are clear signals in the text that indicate that a coming statement is, or the previous statement was, a problem; but (another problem!) occasionally there are no such signals.

Recognising Unsignalled Problems in Texts

If we read that someone has sat on a nail, we would have no difficulty in understanding that he has a problem – which presumably calls for a solution. However, if we read that he has sat on a chair, there is no such problem. The individual words taken separately do not tell us that the first action is a problem and the second is not; we have to understand the whole sentence as representing a problem. The importance of being able to recognise what is a problem and what is not can be seen from this simple pair of actions. For the problem, remedial action is necessary, and we would expect to read about it in the text. If there were no mention of a solution to the problem given in the text, we would think it very odd indeed and would have sound grounds for criticising the text as having an inadequate prose structure. For the action that is not a problem, however, there is no such need for a description of the solution, and the text will continue in a different way. Thus the direction of continuity of the text can be seen to depend on whether something is a problem or not.

Even if the chair were rusty, sitting on it might or might not create a problem. There would be no problem for a carpenter in working clothes eating his lunch, but it would be a problem for a lady in a new white evening dress – and we would again expect appropriate expressions of horror and attempted action to remove the rust stains. Thus the situation often has to be taken into account in deciding what is a problem and what is not. If, for example, a journal is published a little later than usual, this delay will not materially concern many recipients of the journal. But it may be of great concern to readers answering advertisements for professional positions, as shown in Example 38. This text is a formal announcement (note the very formal *Readers are advised*) instead of the more informal use of *you* and *your* seen earlier. The two verbs *advised* here mean to give advice and to inform, respectively.

Example 38   A Situation as a Newly Recognised Problem

Closing Dates

From time to time readers receive their copy of this journal/newspaper close to the closing date for applications printed in the advertisements. Readers are advised to reply to a job advertisement in these circumstances and tell the advertiser that the journal/newspaper was delayed. In cases of late publication, the advertiser will have been advised by the publisher and in general advertisers are willing to co-operate.

(*Chartered Mechanical Engineer*, April 1979, p. 118)

The first sentence presents the situation that from time to time readers receive their copy close to the closing date for answering advertisements in the journal. For those wishing to reply to an advertisement, this situation can be seen to present a problem as they may be unable to reply before the closing date for the job they are interested in. The solution recommended is that they should apply anyway, telling the advertiser that the journal was delayed. The final sentence is an evaluation of the recommended solution as it indicates that advertisers have been informed of the delays and will generally co-operate – meaning they will probably extend the closing date.

Other examples where we have to interpret a situation as creating a problem have already been cited. Example 5 includes a situation for Sally which we recognise as a problem by her affirmation *Yes* and by *Peter's teething*, and *I was up all night with him*. In Example 8 we see that the writer has a problem with her man's spare tyre. Other examples in earlier chapters have specific signals that indicate that there is a problem, however. Example 9 clearly states that retaining the growth of greenery *can sometimes be a problem*, Example 28 indicates *a great difficulty*, and Example 12 includes problems as we learn that the coypus have been *destroying crops and damaging drainage systems*. Words such as *problem* and *difficulty* obviously indicate a problem whenever they occur in a text. However, words like *destroy* and *damage* can indicate a problem or a solution, depending on what is being destroyed or damaged.

Clear Signals of Problem

The clear single-word signals that indicate problem will become more apparent throughout the book. Obviously words like *problem*, *difficulty* and *snag* tell us that there is a problem, but so do the negatives *unavailable, incompatible* and *inadequate*, and the words *smelly, stain* and *corrosion*, and the words of quantity *not enough, lack* or *too*. A list of the problem-signalling words and groups of words found in the examples of the book is given in Index J and you should at this stage look at that index and start becoming familiar with the overt signals of problem. In Example 39 see if you can identify the exact words that indicate problem. Note the effective use of the active and passive in this formal text.

Example 39   Problem Followed by Solution

'Clean' Electrical Power Systems

1 Studies of transient disturbances in electrical power systems and maintenance records of machines and equipment revealed that variations were adversely affecting electronic control systems at the Oak Ridge Y-12 Plant operated by Union Carbide's Nuclear Div. for the U.S. Atomic Energy Commission. For example, large or fast voltage changes often experienced with conventional power systems can trigger the logic circuits of control systems causing erratic operation or downtime.
2 To eliminate these problems, 'clean' electrical power supplies of the flywheel ride-through generator type have been installed to isolate the electronic portions of numerically and computer controlled machines and equipment.

(*Manufacturing Engineering and Management*, May 1974, p. 21)

It may not matter that transient variations are affecting electronic control systems, but it does matter that they are being *adversely* affected. Details of the situation which these studies were conducted to examine are given in the same sentence. The example given in the second sentence indicates a specific problem as we are told that large or fast voltage changes cause *erratic operation* or *downtime*. The solution is given next, clearly indicated as such by the introductory *To eliminate these problems*.

The length and complexity of the subjects of all three sentences are a major contributory factor to the maturity and formality of the style of this example.

It is possible to recognise almost anything as a problem that is erratic, expensive, inefficient, smelly, unstable, cumbersome, inadequate, noisy, inaccurate, and so on. These are all words that usually indicate that something is 'bad' in some way and things and situations characterised as 'bad' are problems that one hopes can be overcome. Note how the signals help us to recognise the problem in Example 40 and thus enable the reader to understand the structure of the text. The personal pronoun *I* and the dash indicate some informality, and this is balanced somewhat by the more formal passive constructions in the second paragraph.

Example 40   A Full Structure with Clear Signals of Problem

Pipe Bender

1   When bending 15mm and 22mm copper pipe during the installation of my central heating system, I found that although the use of internal bending springs prevented the tube from collapsing, it was difficult to get the degree and position of the bend just right – especially near the end of a length of pipe where it was almost impossible to get enough leverage to bend it over the knee.
2   The simple pipe bender is made as shown, from a piece of 25mm thick timber, cut to the marked radii. The two halves can be held in a wide-opening vice, or ideally, between the plastic wedges of a Black & Decker Workmate workbench. By placing the pipe between the formers and gradually tightening, a neat, precise bend can be made.

(*Practical Householder*, May 1980, p. 14; an illustration accompanied this text)

The normal problem with bending copper pipe is that of the pipe *collapsing* or 'buckling'. This was not a problem when internal bending springs were used, but that solution to the general bending problem was not adequate for bending pipe near the ends – note the use of *although* to signal the contrast between adequate use and inadequate (problematic) use of the internal bending springs.

The problem, even with the bending springs, of bending near the ends of pipes is indicated by *although*, by *difficult* and finally by *almost impossible*, which takes difficulty a little further.

The first two sentences of the second paragraph tell us about the solution. The final sentence tells us how the solution works; it also provides some evaluation in that *a neat, precise bend can be made*.

Although the first sentence is very long indeed, the clear structure (signalled by *When* and *although* and helped by the commas) and the break with the dash make it very readable.

In Example 40 the usual solution to the pipe bending problem was seen to be inadequate for bending near the end of the pipe; this inadequacy was a problem which needed to be solved, and the simple pipe bender provided the answer. We shall now examine information structures involving such deficiencies with existing solutions, and their improvement.

Deficiency with an Existing Solution

Quite often there already exists a solution to the problem specified. If that solution were adequate, there would not be a problem to write about and so the writer often needs to explain why an existing solution is not adequate. This involves introducing into the text the 'old' solution together with an evaluation of its deficiencies as shown in Example 41. The writer is stressing the features of the new drill press in a fairly formal style.

Example 41   Inadequacy of the Old Solution

On-Site Drilling

1   Manual on-site large capacity drilling of heavy gauge steel is almost impossible, especially if the job is overhead. The solution in the past would be to take the work piece to a pillar drill, a time-consuming and awkward solution to say the least.

2   The problem was solved with the development of the Portable Electromagnetic drill press which can clamp itself to the work piece.

3   With a magnetic hold value of 2,400 lbs on 10 mm thick material, the rack and pinion feed system allows smooth accurate drilling with minimum effort from the operator. In addition, a 2-stage switch allows the press to be positioned before switching on the full magnetic hold and the unit is equipped with a safety chain, in case of a power failure.

(*The Plant Engineer*, March 1979, p. 18)

The situation is given in the title, which (in the context of the article from which this was taken) tells us that we are concerned with drilling steel members on the construction site. The problem to be considered is identified as manual on-site large capacity drilling of heavy gauge steel, and we know this is a problem because we are told that it is *almost impossible*.

Next comes the *solution in the past*, followed by its evaluation as being *a time-consuming and awkward solution*. Because of the existence of this deficiency in the old solution, the problem still remains to be solved in a better way.

The second paragraph tells us that *The problem was solved* and how it has been achieved. We can tell from the details provided that the new solution not only solves the problem, but does so in a way that avoids the deficiencies inherent in the old solution. The final paragraph provides details of the new solution. Two minor problems are solved in the final sentence: the need to allow the press to be positioned before the full hold is switched on, and the possibility of power failure.

Note, in the final sentence, how the drill press is referred to first by the partial repetition *the press* and then by the superordinate general noun as *the unit*; this ensures clarity and variety.

In persuading readers of a need for their products, advertisers may have to explain deficiencies in competitive products. That is, because of brand loyalty and the reluctance of many customers to change without a good reason, advertisers may have to provide that reason. They often do that by pointing out deficiencies in the usual solution adopted by customers (see Example 42). This text exemplifies the language of sales; note, for example, the use of the dash and adverbials at the end of paragraph 4 to stress the advantageous qualities of the product.

Example 42   Deficiencies with Existing Solution Recognised and Overcome

1 Whatever the colour of our hair, most of us fancy a change now and then. The trouble is that most chemical dyes will probably harm your hair to some degree, quite apart from the increasing number of links now being discovered between certain hair dyes and carcinogenic and allergic reactions.
2 Nevertheless, dull mouse and boring brown are unlikely to turn many heads and you may be forgiven for desiring a more dramatic crowning glory.
3 Natural camomile and henna have been used for centuries to improve hair colour and condition, and you can use them too. Camomile will gently lighten fairer heads of hair and henna will add red highlight.
4 You could use the old-fashioned method – both camomile flowers and

natural henna are still obtainable – but there are some non-synthetic shampoos incorporating natural plant dyes available from Klorane, and if used regularly, these should achieve the desired effect – gently, gradually and without harming your hair . . .

(Slimming Naturally, April/May 1980, p. 7)

The statement that *most of us fancy a change now and then* (to hair colour) is a simple need, a type of problem discussed in the next chapter. The usual solution that achieves that need is to use chemical dyes, but now we are told of the *trouble* with those chemical dyes: they could *harm your hair* (clearly a problem) and could also cause or help to cause cancer or allergic reactions (again problems).

The second paragraph reinforces the need to change hair colour, and therefore for a solution that does not have the deficiencies of the existing methods. Details of the new solution (natural camomile and henna) are then provided. This new solution is evaluated in terms both of whether it meets the original problem (change in hair colour) and also whether it overcomes the deficiencies of the chemical dyes. The evaluation comes at the end of the fourth paragraph.

A tone of empathy and understanding is achieved first by *most of us* and then *you may be forgiven*, and the intimate tone is reinforced by the use of *you* and *your* throughout the text. Readers of this magazine will appreciate the significance of *non-synthetic* and *natural* in the fourth paragraph.

Improvement as a Solution to a Problem

We have already seen that anything that is 'bad' represents a problem, but now we have to extend that understanding by realising that even something that is 'good' can still have a problem associated with it if it can be improved. That is, something may be good, but if it can be improved we have to recognise a problem which is solved by the improvement.

Standards of expectation are continually increasing and what may have been good enough a few years ago may no longer meet the higher expectations; it thus has deficiencies that need to be overcome. Texts reflect the stimulus to improve what exists in some significant way – or to solve a problem in a better way. This concept of improvement as a solution to an implicit problem helps us to understand Example 43, which gives a sufficiently complete account in a single sentence.

Example 43   Improvement as a Solution to an Implicit Problem

Improved Protection Pad

In future, all the mild steel backing plates in the existing range of Klingerflon Duplex ptfe slide bearing pads will be coated with the corrosion protective Klingercoat 40 which will give protection against the most demanding conditions, particularly where the pads are otherwise susceptible to highly corrosive elements such as salt water and spray.

(*Production and Industrial Equipment Digest*, April 1977, p. 7)

There must have been a problem with the existing range of bearing pads, as the title states that the new pads will provide *Improved Protection*. The limitations of the existing range of bearing pads are identified in the second part of the sentence where it is pointed out that the new pads give protection in *demanding conditions*, particularly salt water and spray environments – conditions for which presumably the existing types are not entirely suitable.

This is another long, well-structured technical sentence. Compare the use of the comma here with the use of the dash in Example 40; the comma is less emphatic and more formal.

The improvement is the solution to the deficiency in the previous or existing product, and this improvement can be seen as the significant differences between the old and new products. Where the old and new products are alike there is no improvement or solution to the deficiency of the old product. Where, however, there is significant difference between the old and new product, then that difference can constitute the solution to the deficiency of the old product. In other words, what is inadequate or inefficient in an old product can be overcome by a new product which thus solves the problem. In Example 44 the difference is seen as the solution to the old product. Note how detail of the Lamigrip is compressed within the subject of the first sentence.

Example 44   Similarity and Difference, with Difference as the Solution

Resealable Laminate Pouches Keep Moisture Out

[1]The Lamigrip flexible, fully reclosable laminated pouch incorporates a similar sealing mechanism to the Minigrip range of polythene packs. [2]Unlike the Minigrip, however, the Lamigrip pouch is made from laminated materials. [3]Whereas, therefore, the low density polythene of the Minigrip pack made it unsuitable for goods of a hygroscopic nature, or otherwise vulnerable to moisture or gas, the Lamigrip pouches are suitable for such applications . . .

(*Production and Industrial Equipment Digest*, April 1977, p. 3)

The similarities (signalled by *similar*) between the existing Minigrip and the new Lamigrip are given, and obviously there would be no reason for introducing the Lamigrip if it had no differences. The differences come next (signalled by *Unlike* and *however*), which are crucial to the understanding of the reason for the design of the Lamigrip. The use of laminated materials for the Lamigrip must provide a solution to a problem with the Minigrip – otherwise there would be no need for the laminated material. The details we can predict come next.

We learn that the Minigrip is *unsuitable* for the storage of hygroscopic materials because of its *low* density and this is contrasted with the *suitable* use of the Lamigrip. The use of the laminated material in the Lamigrip solves the problem with the Minigrip, and thus makes the Lamigrip suitable for storing hygroscopic materials.

The cohesion between the clauses and sentences repays close study. In the second sentence the subordinate verbless clause *Unlike the Minigrip* is contrasted with the main clause that follows, and *however* contrasts the differences in sentence 2 with the similarities in sentence 1. Similarly, *Whereas* contrasts the subordinate clause (up to *or gas,*) with the main clause that follows, and *therefore* shows that the information in sentence 3 results from the information in sentence 2.

Change in Situation or Circumstances

Whenever we compare an 'old' system with the new one that supersedes it, there is an implication that the earlier system was deficient in some way and therefore needed to be improved. There may be no need to include detailed discussion of the actual problems with the earlier system either because readers will be familiar with these deficiencies or because they become apparent through the details of the differences between the old and the new. As it is the differences that are solutions to the problems of the earlier system, readers can often work out quite easily for themselves what problems have been overcome by the new system. This is seen in Example 45, which describes the introduction of a new law. From the many comparisons of detail between the old and the new laws, we can understand the differences between them. We can also understand the perceived deficiencies in the old law and the remedies offered by the new one. Compare the style of this text for professional readers with Example 1 which describes a change in a law to the general public.

Example 45   Old and New Laws Compared, with Implicit Problems Overcome

New Law in Louisiana for Married Couples

1   [1]A new community property code came into force in Louisiana at the beginning of 1980, taking away from husbands their previous unique status as 'head and master' of the household. [2]Under the old law, a husband could sell family property, such as the house of car, without bothering about his wife's approval. [3]Now the wife is an equal financial partner in the marriage, and must agree to any transactions affecting family property. [4]However, all property earned during a marriage is community property, and that includes the wife's pay cheque. [5]Previously she could keep it for herself alone.

2   [6]The new law allows married couples to enter into marriage contracts specifying the parties' financial rights, and they may sue each other. [7]The old law allowed parties to sue only after a legal separation, and even then only on property matters.

3   [8]Legal damages awarded to either party are not community property. [9]In the past, damages awarded to the husband were community property, but the wife alone was entitled to any damages awarded to her.

(*Professional Administration*, April 1980, p. 30)

The first sentence is a summary, introducing the new law and indicating in general terms what the new law does in relation to the old.

Sentences 2 and 3 are coupled with *Under the old law* and *Now*, where it is seen that the previous rights of the husband to dispose of family property have been removed. The underlying problem here was the perceived inequity of the old situation, and this has now been remedied.

The *However* indicates the contrast between the husband's loss (sentences 2 and 3) and the wife's loss (sentences 4 and 5). Sentences 4 and 5 are in the form 'Solution–Problem'. There is a perceived inequity in the old law in that *Previously* the wife could keep all her earnings for herself while the husband was expected to support the whole family from his earnings.

In the second paragraph we are told that the new law confers new rights with regard to marriage contracts. The unrestricted right to sue given under *The new law* is compared with the restriction of *The old law*. Thus the old law was again seen to be deficient in that the right to sue was severely restricted, and the new law remedies that deficiency by allowing more civil action.

The final paragraph is again in the structure of 'Solution–Problem'. *In the past*, there was a perceived inequity in that the wife could keep any damages awarded to her, *but* the husband had to share his. This discrepancy has been removed by making damages awarded to either party their personal and not community property.

In Example 45 changes in society and changes in people's attitudes have altered the situation regarding marriage and the respective rights of marriage partners after break-up of the marriage. No mention is made of the situational changes in society that have led to this new law, and it is not necessary as we all know and understand those changes. In essence, the new law is a revised solution to a changed need in society. No evaluation is offered for the new law – that is something we can make for ourselves.

Changes are not always brought about by the recognition of a 'problem' in what already exists. The need may have changed instead, so that what exists no longer meets the new requirements. In other words, something that is adequate under one set of circumstances may be found to be wanting when the circumstances change. The situation and problem can change for many reasons, but one clear cause of such a change occurs when a law or requirement is altered in such a way that an existing product no longer meets that requirement, as in Example 46. The long initial subject and *have dictated a need* indicate a formal style; this text is intended to promote the new Ductape.

Example 46   Change in Situation and Problem Requiring a New Solution

Fire Resistant Ductape

1   Increasingly stringent European fire regulations and recommendations have dictated a need for improved fire resistance for self-adhesive tapes used to seal ducting. Fire resistance is particularly relevant where the ducting leads from one room to another in an office, or from one department to another in a factory.

2   To meet existing regulations and recommendations for the foreseeable future, Arno Adhesive Tapes Ltd. has developed a new Ductape under the name ArNOflame C 516. This flame-retardant Ductape offers similar performance characteristics to the existing well-proven range of Arno Ductapes, combined with fire resistance and self extinguishing flame performance.

(*The Plant Engineer*, March 1979, p. 14)

We are told in the first sentence that the fire regulations have been made *Increasingly stringent*, and this creates a specific problem: *a need for improved fire resistance for self-adhesive tapes used to seal ducting*. Whereas the *existing well-proven* range of Arno Ductapes was satisfactory under the earlier regulations, it does not meet the new ones, and the new ArNOflame C 516 Ductape has been created to meet the new requirements. The difference between old and new tapes is made clear to us in the last sentence where we learn that the new tape has *similar performance characteristics* to the old tape, but in addition has the necessary *fire resistance and self extinguishing flame performance*.

Improvement and Time Change

Inherent in the concept of improvement is the associated change in time. At the point in time of the description, we can look back in time and say that *previously* a problem existed and *now* that problem has been solved. Later on the 'new' product could become the 'old' one, of course, when someone else recognises that it too can be improved and produces something better; we are thus in a state of constant change where there is a continual stimulus to recognise and overcome problems as the basis for general improvement. In Example 47 you will see that previously something was not possible (a problem, of course), but that now it is. Note how the order of the first sentence has been inverted to avoid the otherwise over-long subject; also note the careful use of *the company says* in paragraph 2 to indicate the origin of the information.

Example 47   Improvement from Previously to Now

New Lens

1   Just introduced to the market from a Watford company are coated polycarbonate prescription safety lenses with a scratch resistant coating.
2   Previously, because of the method used to mould and coat polycarbonate, it was not possible to polish and grind the surfaces to produce different optical powers. But now, the company says that it can make the new lens for users of single vision lenses in a range of powers suitable for most prescriptions. Within about six months, they hope to extend the range to include bifocal wearers.
3   The product can meet British Standard impact test grade 2, which means that the lens can withstand the impact of a ½″ diameter steel ball moving at 102 mph . . .

(*Safety*, January 1979, p. 25)

The first paragraph tells us about a new lens, but tells us nothing about its significance as a product. We see the significance in the next paragraph where we are told that *Previously* it was not possible to polish and grind the surface to produce different optical powers, but *now* it can be done. Note the use of *But* as a signal to indicate a change in the type of information being provided.

The first sentence is inverted from the usual order of 'Coated polycarbonate prescription safety lenses . . . have just been introduced . . .'. The inversion places stress on the introduction, which is an important part of the message of the article.

It may not be possible to improve on a solution to a specified problem as far as its actual performance is concerned, but improvement may still be possible by making it available more readily, or at a lower price. Note how, in Example 48, the whole point of the description is to stress the fact that motor units are *now* available. The final sentence illustrates two methods of introducing something: the 'existential' *There*, and the passive *is provided*.

Example 48 Increased Availability as an Improvement

Electric Motor

VWM industrial electric, and geared motor units are now available in the UK through Torvale Transmissions Ltd. The company is offering a service to industry which will provide for quick delivery where urgent replacement is required. There is a complete back-up for spares and maintenance, and an application advisory service is provided . . .

(*Production and Industrial Equipment Digest*, April 1977, p. 7)

We can assume from the first sentence that these motor units were not previously available in the UK, and we can recognise this lack of availability as being a problem for designers and procurement officers. That problem has *now* been overcome. In addition to making the motor units available, the company is also offering a fast replacement service and the necessary spares and maintenance service.

Problem Recognition as the Basis for Improvement

It is well known that there is no chance of curing an alcoholic until he has accepted that he has a problem and is seeking help. Problem recognition is at the heart of all problem-solving activities, for without a problem there can be no problem-solving activity. Because of this, the recognition of a problem can be an important message in its own right even though a solution may not yet have been devised. In Example 49 the solution is so obvious it does not need to be stated, except rather jocularly in the title, which relies on idiomatic use for the double meaning.

Example 49 A Deficiency Seen as a Warning

Don't Be Suckers!

Dear Sir,
I was enjoying Graham Dixey's article, 'Figure Painting Techniques: Part Two,' until I noticed the recommendation of forming a point on a paint brush by putting it to the lips after the brush had been immersed in turpentine. Turpentine is a highly toxic solvent which can damage many organs in the body. The chronic ingestion of even small amounts of this chemical by creating a point on a paint brush does not seem to be worth the risk of the artist.

(*Military Modelling*, February 1980, p. 161)

The recommendation the writer is referring to is seen to be inadvisable because turpentine is *highly toxic* and can *damage many organs in the body*. His conclusion is that the practice is *not . . . worth the risk*. The word *until* signals the end of the enjoyment and the start of the problem. The final sentence has a very complex subject which is associated with the topic *turpentine* by the general substitute *this chemical* included within it.

Usually an alternative solution is suggested when a serious deficiency is discovered with an existing solution. The danger and the remedy are made very clear in Example 50, in which the negative imperative *Never drink* indicates the solution.

Example 50   Serious Danger and Remedy

Cup Crisis

1   Never drink lemon tea from a polystyrene cup because the chemical combination of tea and lemon dissolves the material of the container. This discovery was made by Dr M Philips at the University of Connecticut Health Center. Amazed that his cup was dissolving before his eyes, he performed experiments which showed that lemon juice corroded the cups.
2   In laboratory animals soluble polystyrene is known to be cancer producing, so Dr Philips advises that lemon tea drinkers stick to bone china cups.
(*Family Circle*, June 1980, p. 14; from *New England Journal of Medicine*, vol. 301, no. 10, p. 1005)

The first sentence contains a strong recommendation to avoid a danger followed by the danger as the reason (signalled by *because*) for the recommendation. Details of the danger and its discovery are given in the next two sentences.
    The second paragraph indicates the possible serious nature of the problem followed by the suggested remedy to avoid the danger.
    Note the dramatic effect of *dissolving before his eyes*; the original source of this information would not use such language.

Texts can describe how problems can be discovered through statistical analysis of data. Once it is known that injury or death is caused under certain specifiable situations, it becomes possible to provide details of a solution. This is demonstrated by Example 51. The new regulations are signalled by *are to be, must* and *have to*.

Example 51   Danger Discovered and Solution Being Implemented

Danger of Tyre Explosions

[1]Statistics kept by the Occupational Safety and Health Administration of the US Labour Department show that from 1968 to 1975 at least 22 workers were killed by tyre explosions while they were inflating the tyres. [2]The tyres involved are those generally used on trucks and buses, and mechanics are to be protected by new regulations issued by OSHA. [3]Over 300,000 workers are said to be installing such tyres, and they must all be trained in the proper procedures. [4]Nearly 80,000 filling stations and workshops will have to fit special equipment designed to protect their employees.

(*Professional Administration*, April 1980, p. 30)

Details of the discovery of the source of *Danger* are given in the first sentence. The source of the danger is clarified in the second sentence, and the new regulations are seen as the solution now being implemented. The words *killed* and *explosions* signal problem, and the situation is limited generally to trucks and buses in the first part of the second sentence.

The magnitude of the problem and some details of the new regulations are given in the last two sentences.

Questions
1   What is the structural significance of a statement that represents a problem compared with one that does not?
2   Is it possible for a described situation to be seen as a problem by one reader and not by another? Explain.
3   Why can a deficiency with an existing solution be seen as a problem? Why is this often important in analysing texts. Explain the concept of improvement in terms of the problem and the solution.
4   How does the concept of improvement relate to the differences between products when the problem is solved by modification of an existing solution? Why are signals of similarity and differences significant?
5   How can descriptions of a change in circumstance (situation) structure a text by signalling the creation of a problem?
6   Explain the structure describing the relationship between improvement and time change. What are typical signals of improvement through passage of time?

Examples for Exercises
Here are a few hints on the structures to look out for in the examples that follow. Plenty of examples have already been given to illustrate the specific and implicit signalling of problems, so only texts dealing with improvement and problem recognition are given here.

53   *Improvements*   This is part of a large article. The general statement of improvement is followed by a specific example in which there are clear deficiencies and improvements.

53   *Draught Excluder* Price was a deficiency with the existing solution. Note the evaluation at the end and the interesting stylistic indications throughout the text.
54   *Pearlcorder SD Series* The performance of the basic SD is adequate but it was deficient in not having certain facilities.
55   *Reduction in Spray* A condensed structure describing an improvement in a situation.

Example 52

Improvements

1   I have rarely come across a building where it is not possible to increase usable space by 20 to 25 per cent. If you are imaginative almost anything is possible and this is where the designer can be invaluable to companies. Even buildings erected as recently as the late fifties, or early sixties, can be much improved . . .
2   Another client, Associated Newspapers, needed a facelift for the editorial floor of the *Daily Mail*. The grey, dingy and rather disorganised floor of Northcliffe House will be enlivened this year with bright colour schemes in red and green. The hotch-potch of scattered offices and cubby holes whose proximity to one another bears no relation to their individual roles is being replaced by a planned re-grouping. I was struck by the lack of showmanship; for example, the success of exclusives was rarely if ever proclaimed to colleagues. There were few notice boards, and none dealt with scoops. Display panels will be used to line the editorial corridors with details of big stories, and award winning photographs . . .

(*Professional Administration*, March 1980, p. 20)

Example 53

Draught Excluder

1   The recent windy weather gave me a draughty reminder of the gaps beneath my living room doors. Draught excluders were the answer – but what a price! After a brief examination of the proprietary brands on sale I decided to make my own.
2   A visit to the local car breakers produced a supply of chrome trim strips at the modest cost of 10p each. I cut a length of this to suit the width of the door and drilled holes through it at approximately 150 mm (6in) intervals. The actual draught excluder was a suitable length of Pirelli rubberised webbing, as used in furniture upholstery (approx. 50p per metre). The webbing is merely fitted beneath the chrome strip and the whole thing screwed to the bottom of the door, so that it just touches the floor. Not only is this arrangement neat and attractive, but it is also highly efficient . . . and cheap.

(*Practical Householder*, May 1980, p. 14)

Example 54

Pearlcorder SD Series

OLYMPUS have expanded their SD series of Pearlcorder SD micro-cassette recorders to include the SD2 and SD3 models. The SD2 matches the performance of the SD, but incorporates a choice of speeds. A speed selector switch changes operation from the standard 2.4cm/sec for one hour per microcassette tape, to 1.2cm/sec providing two hours per tape. The SD3 incorporates a micro-computer providing a variety of functions. It incorporates a multi-function quartz digital display which acts as a tape counter, clock, timer and stopwatch.

(*Industrial and Commercial Photographer*, June 1979, p. 116)

Example 55

A reduction in spray dangerously thrown up from wet roads by trucks is claimed by Monsanto for its new Clear Pass: a combination of flaps and valances that 'traps the water and reroutes it back to the road surface'.

(*Sunday Telegraph*, April 1980, p. 8)

Chapter 6

Recognising Different Problems in Texts

The Broad Scope of Problems

An important key to being able to recognise structures in texts is the ability to recognise signalled problems. The term 'problem' is not being used in the rather limited sense of a chess problem or a mathematical problem, but in a much wider sense as meaning any form of un-happiness, discomfort, annoyance, or dissatisfaction with something or with a situation. All problems are recognised as being adverse evalua-tions, and this is a topic discussed in more detail in Chapter 8. This chapter is concerned with broadening your understanding of different types of problem and the linguistic signals that communicate them.

Index B includes a list of different types of problems to be found in the examples in this book, and a brief examination of the types identified should prove useful at this stage. Later, examination of the examples together with the index can provide the basis for further detailed study of the types of problems if that is one of your educational objectives. A good exercise now is to review the examples covered so far in the book to see if you can classify them into definable groups such as those suggested in Index B. Most of the examples so far can be classified under the headings of: deficiency, or 'not good enough'; something that is unpleasant, obnoxious, un-sightly, annoying, or inconvenient; injury, illness, or discomfort; and too many or not enough of something.

We now need to analyse the use of some of the less obvious (but none the less important) types of problem within prose structures. This chapter concentrates on the signalling of decisions, aims, needs, formal requirements, psychological problems, and the need or desire to know something. Other types of problem are identified in Index B.

Decisions Signalled as Problems

To be or not to be – that is the question. Hamlet had quite a problem when he had to decide whether to live and suffer oppression or to fight the oppression and thus die in the attempt. His soliloquy included a debate about the pros and cons of death and, finding that the potential problems associated with the dreams of death outweighed the advantages of the peacefulness of death, he decided to live and suffer. Decisions of all kinds – from insignificant ones to very important ones – are problems, and they are solved by the decision made. 'Should we move or not?' is the serious question asked in the article from which Example 56 is the abstract and part of the introduction. The part of the article quoted shows that the decision is clearly signalled as a problem, and one of great importance for the companies concerned. The word *too* is used three times to indicate a problem, and the final use is italicised to indicate surprise that anything could be too valuable. Note the double meaning of the title and the informality achieved by the use of the colloquial *right under their noses*.

Example 56   A Decision as a Serious Problem

A Moving Question

Ab For many firms the decision to move may be too drastic, especially when coupled with the risk of staff loss and customer confusion. David Leon FSIAD questions whether some firms really need to move when with a little intelligent help from an interior designer they may find they already have all the facilities they require right under their noses.
1 To move or not to move – this is one of the major problems facing expanding companies as we approach the 1980's. The decision is rendered more complex by many new factors.
2 The ever-spiralling cost of land and property has added a two-dimensional element to the problem. On the one hand, it may be too expensive to purchase a new office or factory. On the other it is now quite conceivable that the property you already occupy may be *too* valuable to justify your remaining there . . .
(*Professional Administration*, April 1980, p. 22)

The abstract points out that the *decision to move* may be *too drastic*, especially when associated with other possible problems – the *risk* of *staff loss* and *customer confusion*. What the author questions is whether companies should choose to move their premises, and this question is asked in the light of the alternative that interior designers could provide a better solution to the need prompting the possible move.

The decision *To move or not to move* is identified as *one of the major problems* facing many companies. The second sentence of paragraph 1 calls the problem *The decision*, also stating that it is now more complex than before. In paragraph 2 a general statement is made about *the problem*, and further details are given.

The two-dimensional element is signalled by *On the one hand* and *On the other*. The expected details of how property can be too valuable follow in the text, of course.

Decisions often involve a comparative evaluation of competing solutions to a problem. In Example 56 the problem is the need for more space, the attainment of which has become an objective. The writer is pointing out that there may be a viable alternative to moving. If the decision to move is made, it could well create problems for the staff as they may not want to move, and this in turn could cause problems for the company. This is what is meant by the *staff loss* mentioned in the abstract. Another possible problem mentioned in the abstract is *customer confusion* which, combined with the staff loss, could be *too drastic*.

Dilemmas and Decisions

When the choices to be made in a decision are equally bad or equally good, the decision-maker is said to be in a 'dilemma'. In Example 57 there are two choices – to increase prices or not to increase prices – where, as with Hamlet, the respective advantages and disadvantages have to be weighed up before a decision is made. In this text the main title (*OIL*) gives the situation and this is followed by a subtitle which gives the problem to be discussed.

Example 57   To Increase or Not To Increase –That Is the Dilemma

OIL

The price problem

1   It is now abundantly clear that Saudi Arabia's attempt to restore order to the world oil market by raising her prices has failed dismally. And there is now speculation that the Saudis, disappointed by the response of their OPEC partners, will raise production to depress the market.

2   Whatever happens in the Middle East, the North Sea pricing dilemma will remain. The price of North Sea crude – arguably out of line with world prices, at $29.75 a barrel, before the recent moves – could easily be raised to as much as $34.35. Comparable Nigerian and Libyan crudes sell for $34.21 and $34.72 respectively. But the British National Oil Corporation is constrained by the Government's unwillingness to be seen as contributing to the oil price spiral. This is despite

pressure from smaller oil companies such as Lasmo and Tricentrol to price at world levels, and the loss of tax revenue of upwards of £500 million a year.

(*Now!*, 8 February 1980, p. 67)

There are two sets of problems in this text. In the first paragraph we are told that Saudi Arabia has an aim, which is *to restore order to the world oil market*, their perceived lack of order obviously being a problem to them. Their attempted solution was to raise prices, but this has *failed dismally*. Their next solution will be to *raise production*, hoping to *depress the market* and thus ultimately restore order to the market – the original objective.

The *dilemma* appears in the second paragraph: whether to increase the price of North Sea oil. Differences between the current price and other prices are given so that we can judge the possible reasonable extent of the increase. The obvious decision is to increase the price. However (note the *But* to signal contrast) the government does not wish to be seen to be adding to the price spiral. On the other hand, there is pressure to price at world levels and not doing so results in comparative 'loss' (compared with what could have been obtained) of a significant tax revenue. So the Corporation has to weigh up the pros and cons of the two choices in the dilemma and make a decision.

There are two anticipatory structures in the first paragraph, containing pre-evaluation (by *It is now abundantly clear that* and *there is now speculation that*) of the main parts of the sentences.

Needs and Aims

The concept of 'need' is an extremely broad one, ranging from quite trivial momentary needs (e.g. for an ice-cream or hamburger) to formally compiled corporate requirements for a specific solution. Within the broad spectrum of needs, we can recognise basic personal needs concerned with hunger and physical protection and the higher needs for love, recognition and security.

A very common basic need for many people is the need to know something. The need-to-know ranges from simple requests for information to intellectual inquiry that stimulates research. Example 58 is a set of 'need-to-know' problems, where the solutions are seen to be the answers to the questions. The extreme informality of this text can be seen from the headings, the use of questions and the incompleteness of the questions (e.g. *Going motoring?* instead of the complete question 'Are you going motoring?'). Such incomplete questions are more typical of speech than writing.

Example 58   Simple Needs and Solutions

Telephone Information Services

Recipes
a.   Cannot think of a meal for tonight? Call the Recipe Phone. Daily recipes for an economical meal for four are recorded by Audrey Ellis, a well known cookery expert.

Weather
b.   Going out for the day? Doing the washing? Check with the Weather Phone first for information supplied by the Meteorological Office.

Keeping time
c.   An important date? Must be on time? The Time Phone can help you by giving the time correct to one twentieth of a second.

Motoring
d.   Going motoring? Call the Motoring Phone for information, supplied by the Automobile Association, covering roads within 50 miles of each centre shown in the Dialling Code Booklet or directory preface.

(Post Office Telecommunications Publicity Leaflet, 1980)

In each of these examples the need is made clear in the question, and a solution is then offered. The general heading was 'Telephone Information Services' (the general situation) and the headings for each item provided the specific situations. There is no evaluation of the solutions as the solutions offered will clearly overcome the need-to-know problems.

Items *a*, *b* and *d* use the imperative for the solution, a technique common in advertising.

An aim or objective is not just a recognition of a problem, but also the decision to work towards overcoming it. Aims can be communicated that spring from any dissatisfaction, ranging from the need for self-expression to the practical determination to overcome a specific problem. Note in Example 59 how a problem has arisen and how the decision has been made to counteract it; this aim will eventually be met by the new standard. The paragraphs are very short, but the writing style is otherwise quite formal.

Example 59   An Aim Seen as a Type of Problem

Hydraulic Fluid Tests

1   To counteract the problem of accidental ignition of fluid in spray form when using hydraulic fluids, the British Standards Institution has

safety, quality, and so on, and also by other organisations who have a complex problem that needs to be formulated, or a problem that needs to be defined for legal purposes. Requirements of both a government authority and companies are mentioned in Example 61.

Example 61   Authoritative Requirements as Formulated Problems

1   Resin products for the completion of two large flooring contracts within the food industry have recently been supplied by Structoplast.
2   On the first contract, 5,200 sq m of Ceemarfloor, epoxy resin based, heavy duty floor topping was supplied to the Rogaland Fellesalg slaughterhouse and meat canning factory in Stavanger, Norway. Ceemarfloor is resistant to the corrosive effects of blood, fat and amino-acids, and also imparts hygienic, easy clean and non-slip characteristics to the floor surfaces. Only Ceemarfloor conforms to the stringent requirements of the Norwegian Health Authority governing the use of resinous flooring systems.
3   The second contract was for over 5,000 sq m of Ceemarcyne con-crete sealer to the floor of a large food warehouse in the UK. The requirement was for a sealer which would resist the corrosive attack of sugar upon a granolithic floor and remain dust free, while being used by forklift trucks. Ceemarcyne non-toxic resin system was applied to all floor surfaces to achieve this chemical resistance.
4   Both Ceemarfloor and Ceemarcyne had been specified to cope with specific problems which would not have been adequately solved by the use of concrete or conventional floor systems alone.

(*Building Specification*, April 1976, p. 49)

The first paragraph is a summary, telling us that there have been two large flooring needs, and that these have been met.

The second paragraph deals with the first contract. The first sentence tells us of the solution as we are told that it *was supplied*; quantities of the product supplied and the name of the company who had this floor-ing need are also given. The second sentence provides evaluative details of the product used. In the third sentence we learn that the product *conforms to the stringent requirements* laid down by the Norwegian Health Authority; it is thus an answer to the needs specified by that authority as well as being an answer to the needs specified by the slaughterhouse. This latter need can be seen from what the product can achieve – as detailed in the second sentence of this paragraph.

In the third paragraph details of the solution (over 5,000 sq. metres of Ceemarcyne) for the second contract are given in the first sentence, and this is followed by details of the *requirement* in the second. The third sentence in this third paragraph tells us that the product was applied *to achieve this chemical resistance,* that is, to meet the require-ment.

The fourth paragraph tells us that the two products *cope* with *problems* that could not be *solved* by other products. This is a comparative evaluation of these two products, positive for these two and negative for the others.

Example 61 is rather complex, involving problem, solution and evaluation for two separate contracts in two different countries. The unity of the text is achieved by the common situational background in the first paragraph and, in the final paragraph, the common evaluation of the products used compared with other products. The overall structure of the text can be seen in Figure 6.

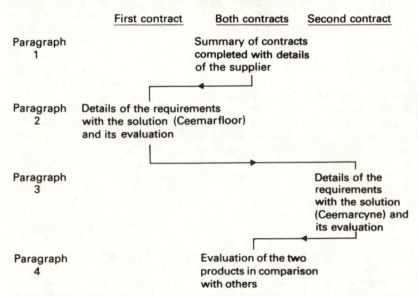

Figure 6 Overall information structure for uses of two products.

A list of requirements laid down by an organisation stipulating such things as quality, safety, standard sizes and test procedures for commonly occurring situations is called a 'standard', and the accepted definition of a standard is that it is a solution to a commonly occurring problem. In Example 61 the need to specify details of effectiveness for resinous flooring systems has resulted from that need occurring many times, and the Norwegian Health Authority requirements meet this need by laying down minimum acceptable levels of effectiveness.

Companies, especially large ones, have their own standards departments which produce standards for commonly occurring problems within their organisations, and industries have developed standards in everything from jam-making to steel production. Each country has its own standards organisation, and groups of countries (e.g. NATO, the EEC) adopt standards for those groups to ensure interchangeability of parts, consistent quality, and so on. Standards change to reflect changing requirements and the changed regulations can make existing products no longer adequate; Example 46 shows how such changes are the motivation for improvement.

Simple needs and formal standards and requirements can now be seen as being at opposite ends of a broad spectrum of needs. At the formal end we are involved with legal documents in business or engineering, and at the informal end we have basic day-to-day simple needs. Related to these simple everyday needs are those arising from psychological problems.

Psychological Problems

Whatever the basis for a person's self-destructive feelings, we have to recognise that someone who is unduly worried or depressed has a problem. There may be no apparent reason for the problem, but it is a problem nevertheless because of the unhappiness caused by the worry or depression itself. The same is true of jealousy, anger, or fear, and we have to regard such natural emotions as problems in their own right whether or not we agree that those affected should have such emotions on the strength of the apparent reasons. There are many signals of psychological problems, some of which can be found in this paragraph.

In many cases, as with terminally ill patients, for example, the cause of the fear cannot be removed, and the counsel given can at best help the patient to accept the problem. Where, however, the basis for worry and anxiety can be seen to be less severe than the sufferer may think it is, an explanation can well help to reduce the worry. Example 62 is based on such an explanation.

Example 62   Reducing Worry through Knowledge and Understanding

Stretch Marks

1 Doctors usually regard stretch marks as trouble free, but their presence can seriously upset a patient and cause depression or marital problems.
2 Stretch marks are, in fact, harmless areas of thinner skin that form in 35% of all adolescents, including 11% of all young men. In men, they occur on the buttocks, over the sacrum and occasionally on the abdomen. In women, the abdomen and breasts are the most common areas to be affected. Blondes are affected as often as brunettes, fat

people as often as thin, and there is no truth in the old wives' tale that women with stretch marks are more likely to tear their skin during childbirth.

3   No treatment has yet been proved to prevent or cure stretch marks and the steroid creams, so useful in some skin conditions, will make them far worse. People with stretch marks need to know that theirs is a common condition; feeling guilty or damaged is a sure way to lead to depression. Above all, other people should give sufferers sympathy and understanding.

(*Family Circle*, July 1980, p. 25; from *British Journal of Sexual Medicine*, October 1979)

The psychological problems of stretch marks are made clear by *upset a patient* and *cause depression or marital problems*, with *but* mediating between the *usually* and *trouble free*, and these problems.

The second paragraph tells us what stretch marks are and where and in whom they occur. The part dominated by *there is no truth in the old wives' tale* denies a myth, thus removing a possible basis for fear. We are also told that stretch marks are *harmless*, and this will help to alleviate the problem of worry.

The first sentence of the third paragraph tells us that there is no known solution to this problem, and states that steroid creams are not a solution (as we might expect) and that they will actually make the condition worse. The solution to the psychological problem is identified in that people *need to know* that this is a common condition. If they *feel guilty* or *damaged*, they could develop *depression*, a psychological problem. A further suggested solution is that others should be sympathetic and understanding.

No meaningful evaluation of the suggested solutions is given as the effect of the suggestions will depend on the individual circumstances of the sufferer and the reactions of friends.

The difference in occurrence between men and women is clearly signalled in the second paragraph by *In men* and *In women*. In the first of these sentences the stretch marks are included by the substitute *they*; in the next sentence, the stretch marks are implicit, with the meaning (by the stretch marks) at the end of the sentence.

'Need-To-Know' Problems

It is natural for us to want to know things, and when we do not receive an answer to our need to know it becomes a problem. 'Need-to-know' problems can range from the simple case where someone wants some readily available information, to instances where researchers devote years of their lives to the discovery of a principle or cause of a problem (e.g. what causes cancer?). The writer of Example 63 had no doubt that his lack of knowledge of a certain topic constituted a problem for him; he actually identifies his lack of knowledge with the word *problem*. Use of the personal pronoun *I* and the idiomatic *gap* of knowledge are typical of personal letters.

Example 63   A Need To Know Identified as a Problem

Sirs,
[1]I have recently become interested in the uniforms of the French army since 1870. [2]While I can find sufficient information regarding clothing and equipment I keep coming up against the same problem – the kepi. [3]Most sources describe the detail on the side of the headgear but I have come across none that adequately describe the devices on the crown. [4]Would it be possible for you to fill in this gap for me? . . .

(*Military Modelling*, February 1980, p. 133)

The writer provides adequate situational detail for us to understand his problem. He has no problem with finding information about the clothing and equipment, but he does have a *problem* with finding information about the kepi. Note the *While* to show the contrast between what is not a problem and what is. In the third sentence, he again uses a no-problem/problem contrast (this time signalled by *but*) to narrow down his actual need-to-know problem. His last sentence asks for an answer to his problem, specifically asking the editors to *fill in this gap* of knowledge for him to overcome his problem.

The dash in this example serves much the same purpose as a colon in this context. What follows it specifies what precedes it.

The need to know more about things and to know them more perfectly is perhaps the greatest intellectual driving force, and it can be regarded as the prime stimulus for dedicated researchers in all fields. The researcher decides what he is seeking to discover (i.e. what problem to solve), and then proceeds to search for it. One such motivation is the well-known 'whodunit' problem of the detective, who needs to know who has committed the crime. Example 64 illustrates this. Note the indications of informal style suitable for entertaining and informing general readers.

Example 64   A 'Whodunit' as a 'Need-To-Know' Problem

Love on Rebound

1   Police were baffled when they were called to a house in which every window had been smashed.
2   They could find no stones or any other missiles inside the home.
3   At last they got a clue. The girl who lived there had just fallen out with her boyfriend.

4 He was John Mitchell, 17, of Canberra – the local boomerang champion. He confessed.

(Weekend, 2–8 April 1980, p. 39)

The need to know is made clear in the first paragraph, where we learn that the police are *baffled*. They looked for the obvious clues, but failed to find them. They then had the *clue* that the girl had *fallen out* with her boyfriend. They concluded that the boyfriend had done it, and this was reinforced with the knowledge that he was a boomerang champion. The final sentence confirms their suspicions.

The structure of the example is situation (the broken windows), problem for police (the 'whodunit'), suggested solution (the boyfriend) and evaluation (confirmation).

The short sentences and short paragraphs give the impression that the information given is a list of major highlights of a complex story – as it probably is.

All informative writing can be seen as a solution to a 'need-to-know' problem. Accounts of football games, discussions of economic trends, reports of the latest war or revolution, reviews of books and plays, highly technical papers in journals – all these and many more meet the needs of readers to be informed about the topic being described. The writer, in attempting to meet the needs of his readers, tries to predict exactly what his readers need to know and he then directs his writing to meeting those needs.

Even street signs and notices are such solutions, and notices can be analysed in these terms and in terms of 'problem' notices (e.g. Steep Hill), 'solution' notices (e.g. Go Slow) and combinations. Examples of English prose usually contain several sentences at least, but road signs do not need to have a written context for us to understand them and so single statements or simply signs are adequate communications.

Questions
1 Define and describe the use of the word 'problem' in its widest sense, giving examples of different types of problem.
2 How can decisions and dilemmas be seen as problems? How does a description of them involve pros and cons?
3 What is an informal method of suggesting a basic need and then answering it? How closely does this relate to usage in speech?
4 What is the prime difference between aims and the problems that initiate them? How are they signalled?
5 What are psychological problems? Should we ignore them on the basis that they have no adequate demonstrable basis? List several words that indicate different types of psychological problem.
6 What are 'need-to-know' problems? Explain the range from simple needs

to an intellectual stimulus for research. Explain several 'problem' road signs in terms of the motorists' need to know.

Examples for Exercises
Here are a few hints on the information structures to be found in the examples that follow.

65 *The Right Handsets* People are asked if they have problems, and then solutions are provided.
66 *Entrance Matting* Aims identified and met.
67 *New Laws Aimed at Better Knowledge* Need-to-know problems recognised to allow identification of other problems followed by remedial action.
68 *Bridging Cavities* A need-to-know problem to avoid a problem is answered.

Example 65

The Right Handsets

1 Have you problems in deciding which of a number of telephones in the room is ringing?
2 Do you receive calls from people who always seem to be whispering? These and associated difficulties can be overcome by fitting special handsets.
3 On one, a built-in lamp flashes to indicate incoming calls, giving instant identification and solving the problem of which bell is ringing.
4 The problem of hearing softly-spoken callers – or those who shout – can be helped by an amplifying handset, with a simple volume control knob.
5 Both these handsets are of particular benefit to people with impaired hearing.

(Post Office Telecommunications, Publicity Leaflet, 1980)

Example 66

1 At the British Library, Lending Division, Boston Spa, Yorkshire, 36 sq m of Type C (closed construction) Tuftiguard entrance matting has been installed to meet the demands of heavy pedestrian traffic. To allow for multi-directional traffic, 10 sq m of the total area consists of 'Chequer laid' Tuftiguard tiles.
2 The library has over 72 miles of shelving and offers a centralised lending service to Universities and other libraries throughout the country.

(*Building Specification*, April 1976, p. 55)

Example 67

New Laws Aimed at Better Knowledge

1 New laws stressing the provision of more information by industry to the Health and Safety Authorities will provide them with knowledge which is 'a prerequisite for effective remedial action where necessary', Health and Safety Commission chairman Bill Simpson said in a speech at Malvern last month.

2 Draft regulations on notification of the toxic properties of new substances, and on 'major hazard' installations, were being prepared, he reminded his audience – already a new law requires the notification of Genetic Manipulation experiments and proposals on improving the reporting of accidents and ill-health at work have already been published . . .

(*Safety*, April 1979, p. 15)

Example 68

Bridging Cavities

My problem is that I want to install a built-in ventilation wall fan through a cavity wall which has foam insulation in the cavity. I would be obliged if you could give me advice on how to avoid the installation becoming a bridge for dampness from the outside wall and any precautions I should take during the installation . . .

(*Practical Householder*, May 1980, p. 12)

Chapter 7

Evaluation Principles

Evaluation in General Terms

Throughout the last few chapters, the concept of 'evaluation' has been mentioned many times as the final part of the four-part structure 'Situation–Problem–Solution–Evaluation'. No attempt has been made to explain what is entailed in 'evaluation' beyond the general meaning that it in some way indicates the effectiveness of the solution – primarily how well the solution overcomes the identified problem. It is now time to deal with evaluation in much greater detail and to recognise its effects on prose structures.

Evaluation means any information presented about something (not just about a solution, as we shall see in this chapter) that tells us how good or bad that thing is, or that is an expression of personal assessment. Evaluation tells us how 'good' or 'bad' something is in respect of various features, such as: its ability to overcome a defined problem, its importance, its solvability (of a problem), its clarity (of an essay), its efficiency (of an engine), its effectiveness (of a law), and so on. That is, everything has certain attributes specific to the class of thing to which it belongs (see Chapter 2) and an evaluation of it can contain information about any of these attributes to tell us how 'good' or 'bad' it is, often in comparison with other similar things. Thus evaluation is a very wide and commonly occurring type of information – and a very important one.

Evaluation can consist of reliable data or non-controversial evidence, or an assessment or interpretation (conclusion) based on that evidence; it can also include elements of experience-based or 'gut-reaction' feelings or opinions about something, and quite often an evaluation will consist of all these things. In this chapter we shall analyse texts that illustrate these types of evaluation, seeing how they interact and learning about their mutual dependence. We shall also examine how a situation (rather than a solution) is evaluated to create a meaningful information structure of 'Situation–Evaluation', and how the basic 'Situation' structure is identified. In Chapter 8 the principles of evaluation learnt in this chapter will be applied to the evaluation of solutions; Chapter 9 contains analysis of examples illustrating evaluation and test procedures.

Two Parts of Evaluation – Assessment and Basis

Most effective evaluations combine assessment with basis, the thinking assessment part being given at least a reasonable basis by the supporting evidence provided. It is possible to have an assessment without the basis being given, and it is also possible to have just the basis with the assessment being left implicit for the reader to make his own judgement. For many evaluations, however, the combination of subjective assessment and objective basis for that assessment is seen to be a clear and sound way of achieving a meaningful evaluation. Example 69 is an evaluation of a book (a book review) in which both parts of the evaluation are combined.

Example 69   Basis and Assessment Combined

Whistler's Mother's Cook Book
Edited by Margaret MacDonald (Elek, £3.95)

[1]Whistler's mother did not spend all her time sitting with her hands folded demurely in her lap. [2]She travelled extensively, brought up her family singlehanded, and cooked for them with verve and relish. [3]Recipes, reproduced here from her cookery notebook (a continuation of one started by her husband's first wife), feature excellent cakes and puddings and a resourceful merging of the best of English and American food.

(*Now!*, 8 February 1980, p. 83)

The purpose of the review is to evaluate the book (i.e. say how good/bad it is), but the first two sentences do not at first seem to be totally relevant to that task. We see the relevance when we read the third sentence. This is the assessment of the book, and that assessment has been made more effective by the basis given in the first two sentences. The second sentence tells us that she cooked with *verve and relish* and that she travelled widely cooking singlehanded for her family. This forms the basis for the complimentary assessment that includes the words *excellent, resourceful* and *best*.

The first two sentences are connected by the structure that tells us what Whistler's mother did *not* do, followed by what she did do.

Occasionally a writer will have what he feels is such an overwhelming case that his assessment becomes unnecessary, and he is content to let the facts (basis) speak for themselves; see Example 70. The tone is curt and business-like.

Example 70 Basis Sufficient without Assessment

As you requested, I have now obtained course evaluations from all 31-226 students. The evaluations (attached) speak for themselves, and I enclose a summary of the responses from Geology students for the Geology Department.

(Memorandum, Queen's University, Canada, April 1979)

This example speaks for itself, providing an assessment of the course evaluations. Use of *all 31-226 students* indicates that the reader is familiar with the meaning of *31-226*, which is the number of a course.

Without a reasonable basis, an assessment can appear as little more than an unsubstantiated claim. Readers usually expect to be given at least some basis for important assessments, together with some indication that more evidence is available should they wish to investigate for themselves and make their own assessment. Example 71 provides that basis. Here the writer exploits a scientific basis to persuade readers to buy his product; in keeping with this approach, the style is different from normal advertising style.

Example 71 Assessment Backed by Summary of Basis

Vitamin Bee . . .

1   Unlike many so called wonder supplements claiming to rejuvenate and reshape your life, pollen is backed by scientific research.
2   Athletes given doses of pollen show increased resistance to infection, improved performances and a faster return to normal after exertion. Pollen contains traces of most vitamins and amino acids but the test results were far out of proportion with the amount of pollen administered. Some factor in the pollen appears to either increase or facilitate absorption of vital elements in the normal diet.
3   The Apiregis Pollen pictured is collected by bees from a pesticide free area of Spain and is available from many health food shops at about £4.50 for one month's supply.

(*Slimming Naturally*, December/January 1980, p. 5; an illustration accompanied this text)

The description is a comparison between pollen and many *so called wonder supplements*, where the stated difference between the evaluations of the two groups of products is that pollen is *backed by scientific research* and the others are not (note *Unlike*). That is, instead of merely claiming without substantiation that pollen is an effective supplement, the writer refers to some evidence on which such a conclusion is based. That evidence, however, is itself an assessment; no firm basis is given here.

The scientific research reported in summary here concluded that pollen resulted in *increased resistance to infection, improved performances and a faster return to normal after exertion.* This is the assessment based on the research work.

Note the disparaging comment regarding competitive products in the opening sentence. The use of *so called* preceding *wonder supplements* and the use of the hypothetical *claiming* belittle these products, and their lack of research backing is implied.

Details of the actual research undertaken to determine the efficacy of pollen are not provided; we have to take it on trust that such research was carried out and that the conclusions reached were soundly based on the *test results* obtained. Some advertisers of pharmaceutical products invite anyone who is interested to ask for a report of the scientific research, and this then forms the detailed basis for the general assessment. Most people, however, will not be able or interested enough to check the scientific work, but they may be impressed by the statement that it has been done. In a technical report readers would expect to be given enough basis for them to judge the validity of the assessments reached; this is an important difference between advertising and technical writing.

This brings us to the importance of the assessment part of evaluation. The basis can only 'speak for itself' for readers who are willing and able to assess the basis (evidence, data) for themselves and this does not include everyone. Looking at the situation realistically, professional people are paid basically for their ability to weigh up the evidence in certain situations, and then to make intelligent assessments and decisions on the basis of this evidence. Where the evidence is insufficient for a reliable assessment, they will clearly say so and either seek the further data needed or else reach only tentative assessments to reflect the incomplete basis available (see Example 100, paragraph 4). Texts describing the procedure to obtain the necessary evidence and thus make meaningful assessments are discussed in Chapter 9. For now we shall examine examples where the evidence available is seen by the writer to be adequate for a meaningful assessment.

The Combined Effect of Subjective Assessment and Objective Basis

For many evaluations the greatest effect is achieved by providing in the text a thoughtful assessment of what is being evaluated together with appropriate data or other evidence as a basis for the assessment. Assessment involves intelligent interpretation of the evidence and is therefore 'subjective', as interpretation of evidence is at least to some extent a personal matter depending on the background experience and attitudes of the assessor. In contrast, the basis is usually 'objective' as it is information that is verifiable in some way (by repeating an experiment, for example). For most evaluations, the ideal is to have both subjective and objective parts to the total evaluation. We have already seen instances of this in Example 69 and also in Example 71. For both of these, the objective data on their own would not provide an adequate evaluation, and the data had to be interpreted for the reader.

This is the basis for the overall structures to be found in any detailed investigation. The actual terms used may be different, but the idea is the same: the investigator finds his data from testimony, or observations, or perhaps measurements, and then he discusses and interprets the data to bring out the significance and thus make conclusions. Example 72 lists some typical main headings to be found in scientific papers; note that there is a section on the collection of data and another section on their interpretation.

Example 72   Typical Headings for Scientific Reports

Introduction	Introduction
Materials and Methods	Experimental
Results	Conclusions and Discussion
Discussion	

(Annals of Applied Biology, June 1969)

Results or observations on their own are not considered to be enough; interpretation of those results is needed to reach meaningful conclusions. In the headings of Example 72 and in the examples just analysed we do not have the interpretation on its own either. The evaluation is not felt to be complete unless there is objective evidence for what is being evaluated and also some meaningful interpretation of that evidence. It is the combination of the two that provides effective evaluation.

The Significance of Figures and Units

In a description of a new product it may not be sufficient merely to provide the objective test results as the reader may be unable to relate these figures to figures from similar products. That is, faced with a set of data about a product, the reader will be unable to make his own meaningful assessment if he does not know how good these data are in comparison with data about other products. To enable the reader to interpret the data for the new product, he may therefore need data for similar products as it is the difference or improvement that forms that basis for the assessment. Example 73 is typical of this. The style is quite formal; note the overt sentence connectives *Also*, *as a result* and *In addition*.

Example 73   Data Given for Comparison to Allow Assessment

New Metal-Halide Lamp Features Long Life and Improved Colour Rendition

1 [1]Claimed to overcome the problems associated with existing metal-halide lamps, a new design, developed in Japan by the Iwasaki Electric Industry Co. Ltd., stabilizes the colours of the various halides employed as the light source by using special rare-earth electrodes. [2]These electrodes promote the initiation of discharge and allow a part of the rare earth to be discharged from the electrode during its operation – a vital consideration for light generation. [3]Also, it controls the behaviour of the light-emitting substances involved, greatly enhancing the stability of the light source and providing a pleasant white light with improved colour rendition.

2 [4]Among other advantages of the use of rare-earth electrodes is that they suppress optical and electrical changes, such as flux deterioration, variations in the colour of the light, and increases in lamp voltage; as a result, the stabilized characteristics of the light source become available over a long period of time. [5]In addition, the life expectancy of the new metal-halide lamp is about 9000 hr as compared with about 6000 hr for a conventional type, and its efficiency is around 87.5 lumens per watt, i.e. about 10% higher.

(*Engineers' Digest*, April 1976, p. 17)

The purpose of this description is to stress the improvement of the new lamp on existing metal-halide lamps. The title includes assessment of *long life and improved colour rendition*, the basis for which is provided later.

The first sentence makes us recognise that the problem being overcome by the new lamp involves improvement compared with existing lamps. The second sentence tells us how the new lamp works and therefore provides details of the solution being described. The third sentence provides further details and then supplies the comparison of *greatly enhancing* light source stability with *improved* colour rendition. The basis for these assessments is given in the preceding sentence, as an understanding of how the lamp works enables readers to accept that the assessments may well be true.

In the second paragraph the *other advantages* are assessments of the new lamp compared with earlier types. The final sentence provides the data of life expectancy as the basis for the earlier assessment of *long life* in the title. As this basis may mean very little to readers on its own, additional figures are supplied (*as compared with about 6000 hr*) to allow the comparative assessment to be made. In the last sentence the significance of the efficiency of 87.5 lumens per watt is made clear by the comparative assessment *about 10% higher*.

The variety of sentence patterns in the first paragraph is worth observing. In sentence 1 there are two non-finite clauses dominated by the verb forms *Claimed* and *developed* to add information about the design in a subordinate manner. In sentence 2 there is an ellipsis of the subject *These electrodes*, and the two main clauses are followed by an evaluation after the dash. Sentence 3 ends with a co-ordinated pair of non-finite clauses dominated by the verb forms *enhancing* and *providing*.

The facts speak for themselves for experts as long as adequate details are given, and generally they will prefer to make up their own minds from evidence given rather than have an assessment 'forced' on them. But the evidence and possible comparison must be adequate for such an assessment, or else the figures will have little meaning.

Skilled Opinion and its Importance

So far we have discussed evaluation in terms of objective, often measurable, data or evidence and personal assessment based on that evidence. Now we have to recognise two other types of evaluation: the type that cannot be justified in any significant way, and the type that relies on a personal gift or skill as basis. These types of evaluation cannot be 'proved' valid or not, and we must rely heavily on the skill (and integrity, of course) of the person providing the evaluation. If he has no skill in the subject he is evaluating, we must classify it as unsubstantiated opinion, and treat it accordingly. The four types of evaluation are shown in Figure 7.

Thus an account of a meaningful evaluation of something, which can be tangible (a product) or intangible (a musical recording), can have three types of evaluation – basis, assessment and skilled opinion. In many instances only the combination of these three types provides an adequate evaluation.

Skilled opinion is often a vital ingredient in the evaluation. Wine-tasters, tea-testers, tobacco-buyers, and art and antique collectors have to rely heavily on their developed tastes as a basis for decisions to buy. Generals in wartime have to make decisions partly on 'gut-reaction' opinions of a situation, and managers have to make decisions partly based on years of experience. Police investigators often 'know' who is guilty long before there is convincing evidence,

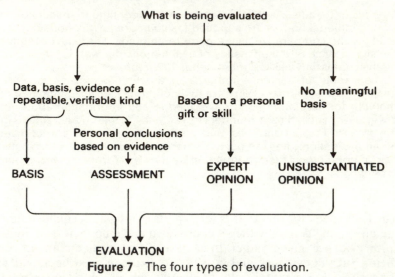

Figure 7   The four types of evaluation.

and experienced chess-players often make moves that they 'feel in their bones' are sound in the circumstances. In all these examples, the decision-makers may not be able to explain fully why they have made that particular decision, and we can rarely expect them to. Note that there are many signals that reflect skilled opinion in the English language.

Impartiality and the Need for Standards

When a skilled person provides an evaluation without giving the basis for his assessment, we have to accept his judgement, and the value of the judgement becomes largely a matter of personal credibility (see Example 74). For the evaluation to be meaningful, the person giving it needs to be skilled in the subject, and we have to assume that he is giving a fair, unbiased evaluation unaffected by personal prejudices. Should we find that an evaluation includes false statements as part of the basis, we have to question the knowledge or integrity of the expert, and the validity of the evaluation is greatly diminished. Where two experts disagree (see Example 77), someone (a judge, for example) may have to assess the relative validity of the evaluations and make a decision on that basis.

Usually we have to trust the person giving the evaluation as being both knowledgeable and fair, and we have to accept the evaluation offered in a text unless we know otherwise. In Example 74 an opera is reviewed; as it is not possible to present much objective basis for the evaluation, we have to rely to a great extent on the skill and impartiality of the reviewer. Note the length and complexity of the sentences in a review intended for intelligent, knowledgeable readers.

Example 74   A Skilled Opinion of an Intangible

The Kent **La Traviata** – Jonathan Miller's production with grey and sepia costumes by Bernard Culshaw after the photographs of Nadar and every traditional cut in the score restored – was not perhaps actually as slow as it seemed and some of the audience at least evidently found the protracted pallors of Jill Gomez in Violetta's death scene affecting enough. She looks the part and adapts her not notably suitable voice intelligently to the role, but partnered by a curiously uninvolved Alfredo from Keith Lewis and surrounded by so "objective" a staging, she was unable to rescue the evening from frigidity.

(*Sunday Telegraph*, 20 April 1980, p. 25)

Overall this is a very negative review. The positive evaluations of the audience reaction and of Jill Gomez are insignificant compared with the slowness, the uninvolvement of Alfredo and the 'objective' staging – all leading to the final assessment of frigidity. In contrast, the assessment of Jill Gomez is quite positive. In spite of *her not notably suitable voice*, she *looks the part* and *adapts her . . . voice intelligently to the role* – but is still *unable to rescue the evening from frigidity.*

Note the effects of the two negative statements: *not perhaps actually as slow as it seems* still means an unacceptable level of slowness, and *not notably suitable* still means something a little less than suitable without meaning completely unsuitable.

There are several points we can learn from Example 74. First, the criticism given is normally assumed to be fair and unbiased, from a legal as well as an ethical point of view. Reviewers are allowed to express their points of view and to have them published even though such reviews could do great harm to box office receipts and artists' careers; the reviewer is providing a skilled, impartial service for his readers, and in providing an assessment of value to the public he has every right to express his views. Only if statements in a text were shown to be deliberately unfair could those adversely affected by such criticism take legal action against the reviewer, the editor of the newspaper and the publishers.

The second point is that the reviewer (in his first sentence) took note of audience reaction in his total evaluation. After all, the opera is intended to entertain the public, and some assessment of how well this has been achieved can be gauged from audience reaction.

However, he quite rightly does not give it pride of place. He brings his own standards to bear and judges in accordance with them. We would not expect a professional cook to judge a plain suet jam pudding on the sole basis of how much children said they liked it (the proof of the pudding is *not* in the eating) any more than we would expect a scholar to produce a text evaluating a course of instruction based solely on student reaction. Relevant standards (e.g. nutrition, scholarship) must also be applied and explained in the text as vital background to any meaningful assessment.

The third – and most important – point about Example 74 is that the basis for assessments are themselves often assessments. For instance, the overall evaluation of frigidity is based, at least in part, on the adverse assessment of one of the artists and of the staging. In texts explaining the judgement of such events as plays, operas and films, little objective basis may be offered for the overall evaluation; the basis has to be largely subjective. Use of an assessment as basis for another assessment is also typically found in advertising.

The Essay: 'Situation–Evaluation'

The basic essay is created when a situation is defined, described and evaluated. Complex essays also include the evaluations from other writers of the same situation together with the writer's comments (often in rebuttal) on those evaluations. One stage further, a thesis or dissertation is the thorough evaluation of a defined situation, where the evaluation is demonstrated in the light of evidence and in the light, perhaps, of earlier contrary evaluations. In all cases, enough of the situation needs to be communicated for the reader to understand what is being evaluated, and the evaluation must be adequately justified. What is adequate justification, of course, depends on the purpose of the evaluation; the requirements in a court of law are more rigorous than the requirements for an entertaining discussion or a point of view.

A common place to find short essays is in the 'editorial' column of newspapers, where the editor comments on the news. It is not his function to report the news – that is done in the reporting columns – and he can thus usually assume that readers have at least some familiarity with the topic he has chosen to discuss. His purpose is to provide his own assessment and skilled opinion of topics of current importance, giving whatever basis or evidence he feels is necessary to convince readers to accept his point of view. Example 75 illustrates this. Note how the text tells us what readers already know with signals: *Last week's decision* . . . and then *of course* in the second paragraph. Note also the emphatic starts to the second and third paragraphs with two 'cleft' sentences: *What . . . are doing* and *It . . . that*. The writer uses *as PW [Procurement Weekly] understands it* to avoid the personal pronoun *I*, thus making the writing more formal.

Example 75 Situation with Positive and Negative Evaluation

1 [1]Last week's decision by five of Europe's leading naphtha consumers to form what is in essence a price information exchange on this most important raw material for their industries can only be welcomed. [2]The price of naphtha on the Rotterdam spot market has been as volatile as the material itself over the last 12 months, and is likely to continue in its present state unless something is done to bring some order into the market.

2 [3]What the five consumers, among them ICI and Bayer, are doing is to pass on information, confidentially of course, on what each is paying for contract supplies of this oil derivative and so be able to compute a 'weighted average' price for each quarter. [4]Such an information flow should enable the major consumers of the material to obtain a more accurate picture of the contract market. [5]They can then go out to intervene in the spot market and to help iron out the fluctuations.

3 [6]However, it is with some regret that we hear that the figures obtained by this naphtha price information exchange are not, as PW understands it, going to be public knowledge. [7]There are many consumers of derivatives of naphtha, particularly in the plastics and petrochemicals industries, who would really like to know what is happening on a contract basis to this commodity. [8]Rotterdam prices have not for a long time reflected the true availability of naphtha in Europe.

(*Procurement Weekly*, 5 March 1980, p. 2)

The first sentence provides an evaluation of naphtha as being a *most important* raw material, and the writer evaluates the decision by commenting that it *can only be welcomed*. The second sentence puts the decision in perspective, indicating that it was taken to overcome the problem of the price of naphtha being *volatile*; the decision to form a price information exchange is clearly intended as a solution to this as it should *bring some order into the market*.

Sentence 3 provides us with further details of the information exchange so that we can understand its possible effectiveness.

Sentences 4 and 5 are projected results assessed by the writer, and these form the basis for the earlier welcoming of the decision. The basis shows how (according to the writer) the new information exchange should work *to help iron out the fluctuations*, which indicates a partial solution. In the third paragraph he expresses his assessed disappointment (with basis) that the information will not be made public; note the signalling of *However* and *regret*.

This example not only illustrates evaluation in action, but also shows that the situation taken for evaluation can also be a solution to something. Writers take as their starting point any coherent group of information, and that information can represent purely a state of affairs, a decision, a law, a product, or quite literally anything. Many of the things and concepts taken for evaluation must have been made for a purpose, and thus to solve a problem. Thus, in evaluating something, the writer often has to make a choice as to whether to introduce the background information (the broader situation and the problem being solved), or merely to treat the 'solution' as a 'situation' worthy of discussion and evaluation in its own right without reference to the reasons for its creation. However, as the prime purpose of most creation is to overcome a definable deficiency or need, the most effective evaluations include discussions as to how well the need has been met.

Writers can and do evaluate anything (i.e. say how 'good' or 'bad' it is in certain respects). Where what is being evaluated is not a solution to a problem (e.g. a person, a scene) or where it is not treated as a solution to a problem, we can recognise the 'Situation–Evaluation' structure in the writing.

Hypothetical Situations

Quite often writers need to evaluate something that is not 'real' as they do not know the true state of affairs; when that happens they have to imagine or suppose something that can be evaluated so that readers have some idea of the basis for evaluation. A particularly common 'hypothetical' situation that is often evaluated is a forecast. We do not really know what the situation will be like in a few years' time, but we still need to evaluate it in order to plan for the future. The solution to this need is to create a hypothetical situation through a forecast of the likely situation in the future, and then to evaluate that situation as the basis for future action (see Example 76).

Example 76   A Forecast as a Hypothetical Situation

Soaring Material Costs Lead to Higher Paint Prices

1   [1]'Very severe' increases in raw material costs will push up industrial paint prices by some 30 per cent this year, the Paintmakers' Association recently forecast. [2]The materials most to blame are white spirit, which rose by 53.3 per cent, and xylol which rose by 38.1 per cent.
2   [3]If the expected increases materialise, it will mean that industrial paint prices have risen by more than 68 per cent in the last two years. [4]And there are signs that the industry is experiencing difficulties in

maintaining sales levels, with the Paintmakers' Association claiming that low cost American chemicals are the reason for higher import penetration.

(*Purchasing and Supply Management*, May 1980, p. 4)

The forecast itself is an assessment (in the first sentence) with adequate basis (in the second). The hypothetical nature of the *forecast* of the first sentence is reinforced by the conditional *If . . . materialise* in the third, and the evaluation of the forecast cost increase is given in terms of the basis only (the price increase). Readers are able to make their own assessment from the figures provided.

The fourth sentence identifies a related problem in that the industry is *experiencing difficulties*; this problem identification is an assessment with basis following *there are signs that* and with what the Association is *claiming* as a *reason* at the end. This forecast and the possible problem the increase is helping to create are presented to readers who will evaluate the new situation as it affects them directly and then take any appropriate action.

Different Evaluations as Disagreements

Quite simply, a disagreement means that two or more people fail to agree on the facts of a matter or, more commonly, on their evaluation of the facts. This is illustrated diagrammatically in Figure 8.

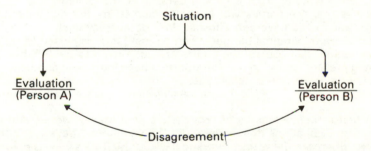

Figure 8   Disagreement as a difference between evaluations.

It is of course quite possible for two people having a difference of opinion simply to agree to differ. This may not always be possible when the issue is important to both people, and where they both feel that, for different reasons, they are right. In scholastic debates, it is usually possible to resolve differences through a detailed analysis of relevant evidence or other data within a commonly accepted theoretical basis (e.g. a mathematical calculation), but the evidence may not always be adequate to provide an unequivocal evaluation on which both parties can agree. Often, there can be no 'right' evaluation or 'wrong' evaluation; each side in a disagreement may have quite reasonable (but different) perceptions of a situation, and each may be able to provide what he feels is adequate basis for his conclusion. This explains the structure of Example 77, which has such a disagreement with opposite evaluations, each with quite reasonable basis.

Example 77   A Disagreement with Both Sides Having Reasonable Basis

Cameras in Court

1   [1]British lawyers may well disagree with the president of the American Bar Association, who has said that cameras in the courtroom were there to stay. [2]Mr. Shepherd Tate told the annual meeting of the American College of Trial Lawyers that the issue was 'not a matter of media versus the bar, but rather the public's right to know'.

2   [3]Television cameras have been allowed at a few trials as experiments, but have not yet been accepted as a matter of course. [4]In fact, the House of Delegates of the American Bar Association does not share the views of the Association's president, and voted against a proposal to permit cameras in courtrooms. [5]There is a strong argument in favour of televising proceedings: the public should observe and learn about their judicial system. [6]The difficulty is that lawyers may have an eye on the camera rather than on the interests of their clients. [7]Mr. Tate believes that the parties will be better served by the openness that electronic media coverage affords. [8]In a democracy such as ours, he said, 'there is potential danger when an institution is closed to public observation'. [9]Of course, the courts are not closed to public observation in present conditions, since reporters have long been allowed in to take notes and report proceedings.

(*Professional Administration*, July/August 1979, p. 29)

The first sentence tells us of two parties who may *disagree*, and the opposite evaluations they have about the situation: whether or not to have *cameras in the courtroom*. The basis for Mr Tate's view is given in the second sentence, the reason being that the cameras are a solution to the *public's right to know*.

The third sentence tells us that there has been no final decision on the matter yet, and in the fourth sentence we learn that an organisation does not *share the views* expressed earlier. This is followed by the prediction of a *strong argument in favour*, with the details coming after the colon to fulfil that predicted information. *The difficulty* signals a coming problem with this idea, and this difficulty is then expressed. This is the basis for the view opposite to that of Mr Tate.

Mr Tate's evaluation (he *believes*) is that open television coverage is preferable, the meaning of *better served* being that the use of TV cameras would be an improvement. Further basis for this point of view is given in the quoted speech in which a *danger* is identified. To rebut this basis, the writer of this report points out in sentence 9 that there is no such danger as courts have long been open to reporters.

There are two examples here of a denial followed by a 'correction' (what is true). They occur in the last sentences of each paragraph and are signalled by *not . . . but rather* and then by *not . . . since*.

Disagreement and Ruling

Eventually, with serious disagreement, someone in authority may have to make a comparative 'value judgement' between the competing points of view and give a ruling on the matter. He may accept one or other of the points of view, or he may impose a view of his own. Such judgements compare the relative 'values' of the two cases and are seen typically in legal cases. They are made only after each side has had a fair opportunity to explain his point of view and to give the basis (or argument) for that assessment. Example 78 describes such a legal ruling. Note how a great deal of important information is compressed within the subject of the second sentence.

Example 78   An Impartial View as an Authoritative Ruling

TV Commercials Need Watching

A lorry driver in the US successfully sued the Ford Motor Co. because his vehicle's chassis was damaged when he drove the vehicle over rough ground. Ford's defence that the damage was not covered by warranty and that they could not be held responsible for abusive use was overruled by the Minnesota judge who accepted the driver's claim that he had merely driven the lorry the way he had seen it done on a TV commercial. The judge's view was that advertising becomes part of the warranty if made for the ultimate purchasers of the product and that the TV commercial would lead the buyer to believe that the lorry could be driven as shown. From this it would appear that claims made in a TV commercial in the US become part of a warranty.

(*Management Decisions*, vol. 16, no. 4, 1978, p. 188: 'Perspectives')

The first sentence gives us the situation of the legal case involving vehicle damage, and we learn that the driver is *successful* in his case. Details of Ford's case come next in the form of basis (*not covered by warranty*) and assessment (*they could not be held responsible*). This is *overruled* by the judge, and we are told that he *accepted the driver's claim*, followed by details of that claim (which is of basis only).

The judge's view is then given; it is in the form of basis or evidence for his ruling, his assessment being his ruling in favour of the driver.

The final sentence is the writer's evaluation as to the likely legal implications of this ruling. This final evaluation is based on the power of legal precedent to be used as a basis for future related legal situations.

The coherence of the last two sentences is interesting. First, the judge's ruling is in two parts, dominated by the co-ordinate pair *The judge's view was that* and *and that*. Both of these parts form the referent for *this* in the final sentence, and thus the words *From this it would appear that* indicate a relation of logical conclusion between the final sentence and both parts of the preceding sentence.

The Information Structure 'Situation'

The purpose of the basic 'Situation–Evaluation' structure is to establish a point of view, and it is very difficult indeed to describe a situation without there being some indication of evaluation in the writing. We have also seen that information containing only details of something may not be what readers need; in fact it will only be suitable if they have sufficient background information to make their own assessments based on the information provided.

The selection of information to be included in a report is itself an evaluation of what the writer thinks is important to his readers, and the order of the information and often even the choice of words and sentence structures provide evaluative information along with the factual statements. We cannot, in this book, delve into all the means whereby writers provide evaluations of what they are describing or how readers interpret information. The point can be made, however, that description without any indication of evaluation or without the reader being led to an evaluation is very rare indeed and is usually only found in very short texts.

Any information presented can be taken as a potential basis for assessment. Even a factual report that a certain dictator has had a group of dissidents executed means to many readers in the West that he is 'bad'. The writer cannot escape that implicit evaluation while still reporting the facts; the facts speak for themselves, whether or not the reporter also includes his own assessment. Example 79 shows clear 'good' and 'bad' factual reporting with implicit evaluation, the two parts being reinforced by the paragraphing.

Example 79   Implicit Evaluation from Factual Statement

1 The dollar continued to benefit from Carter's package (though not Kennedy's primary victories), touching 2¼-year highs, while gold hovered uncertainly. Dollar strength is even allowing America to help

West Germany with its budget deficit: part of the D-mark proceeds of earlier Carter bonds are being placed with Germany's finance ministry.
2 But Wall Street remains in the doldrums. And inflation is still accelerating, the consumer price index soaring 1.4% in America in February.

(*The Economist*, 29 March 1980, p. 85)

In the first paragraph the word *benefit* implies 'good', but even if the word 'climb' had been used instead, it would still be seen as 'good' for the US economy by readers. The use of *even* indicates the writer's surprise (an evaluation) that America is helping the German economy – an unusual occurrence at that time.

But in the second paragraph is a key word, as it indicates the difference of implicit evaluations of 'good' for the first paragraph and 'bad' for the second. The choice of *remains in the doldrums, inflation . . . accelerating* and *consumer price index soaring* all indicate 'bad' evaluations. Note that *1.4% . . . in February* is the basis for the assessment of *soaring*.

'Situation' and its Evaluation

The idea of the 'Situation' structure is that information is supplied to the reader to allow him to make his own assessment. In Example 80 the facts are first presented basically as 'Situation' in such a way that readers can make their own judgement of the matter. This is then reprinted with added evaluation in another publication. There is a noticeable difference in style between the original story and the two commenting paragraphs surrounding it. Use of *that's no April Fool joke* and *quietly consigned it to the compost heap* are colloquial expressions which indicate informal style.

Example 80   Evaluation Added to 'Situation'

Innovation

1 Innovation probably made the United States a super power. It is thus depressing to learn how much the subject has been neglected in North America.
2 In an editorial (Sept. 3/79) *Business Week* said: 'In May 1978 President Carter ordered a sweeping review of federal policies that inhibit industrial innovation. The goal was to modify negative policies and take active steps to stimulate the innovative process. Recommendations were to reach the President's desk by last April 1st. They are still not there, and that's no April Fool joke. A report went to the White House late in the spring, but the President's staff quietly consigned it to the compost heap, and no recommendations have reached the oval office.'

3   For the individual enterprise, it has been said 'innovate or die'. What applies to individual enterprises also applies to the nation.

(Professional Administrator, June 1980, p. 4)

The first paragraph provides pre-evaluation of what is to come, *depressing* and *neglected* being clear signals of how the writer feels. The original information is presented as 'Situation' by *Business Week*, the information being in the form of a failed complete project with a problem (*negative policies*), a goal (to *modify* them), *Recommendations*, and the failure to implement them. The only evaluations are in the *that's no April Fool joke* and the off-hand *quietly consigned it to the compost heap*.

The final paragraph provides an evaluation of the possible repercussions of such failure, the implication being that the US will decline or 'die' if it fails to continue to innovate.

Note that the story of the failure reported in *Business Week* is treated as a 'Situation' by *Professional Administrator*. The point was made earlier that literally anything can be evaluated (even an evaluation) and this means that writers can take any coherent stretch of information and treat it as a basis for evaluation. Thus we can now define 'Situation' as being any coherent stretch of information that is used as the basis or background for thought, discussion, or analysis. The natural and understandable urge for the writer to interpret (at least to some extent) the information he is reporting is clearly seen in Example 81.

Example 81   Overall Conclusion Suggested

Too Lax?

It is easier to get new drugs onto the market in the UK than in America. The British Committee on Safety of Medicines is approached only twice by drug companies – once for a clinical trial certificate and once for a licence, compared with the ten-step American procedure. In the States there is consultation at every stage of research and a drug goes through ten testing phases.

(Here's Health, June 1980, p. 8)

Although there is a comparison between the UK and American systems, the writer refrains from passing an overt judgement in the main body of the text. However, the inclusion of *only* implies that there should be more control, and the title *Too Lax?* is asking readers to consider whether the UK system is strict enough. The writer is not actually making that evaluation, but is suggesting it as a possibility for readers to consider when judging the matter for themselves; that is what the question mark is telling us.

Both *Too* and *Lax* in the title are signals of problem.

Questions

1 What is meant by 'evaluation'? Explain, and give examples of, the four types.
2 Why do writers often need to provide both assessment and basis?
3 In what circumstances would it be appropriate just to use assessment, and just to use basis?
4 Why do some opinions have no definable basis? When is this acceptable and when is it unacceptable?
5 In what circumstances does skilled opinion become vital, and what are the implications for impartiality and the use of standards of judgement? How do these factors affect the analysis of a text?
6 Explain the need for a balanced 'good' and 'bad' evaluation account where appropriate. In what order are these usually found?

Examples for Exercises

Here are some very brief comments about the examples that follow.

82 *The Hidden Ingredients in Bread* Basis for evaluation, but you make the assessment.
83 *Interest Rates: Gloom for Government* Psychological problem with cause, basis, assessment and more basis.
84 *Fisher Dilemma on Fraud* Partial agreement, partial disagreement with alternative, and writer's evaluation. Note the sentence structure in the first paragraph.
85 *6½ Prescriptions Each!* Where exactly are the evaluations?

Example 82

The Hidden Ingredients in Bread

1 Nimble's Farmstead brown bread says on the packet, 'made with 100 per cent wholemeal flour'. So is it okay when you're slimming naturally?
2 Unlike most breads, Nimble carries an ingredients list which shows that as well as wholemeal flour, Farmstead bread contains wheat protein, yeast, salt, shortening, emulsifier, dextrose, malt flour, soya flour and preservative.
3 (Normally you don't know exactly what's been put in bread, for although most bread now comes in a wrapper which could easily carry an ingredients list, bread is still mystifyingly exempt from the food labelling regulations).
4 It comes a bit of a surprise to most people, but all wholemeal bread is allowed to contain emulsifier and preservative – the only two 'additives' on the Farmstead list most people wouldn't recognise as foods (dextrose is just a kind of sugar).
5 So Nimble is as natural as any wholemeal loaf unless you buy from a shop which lists ingredients or can assure you that no non-food ingredients are included. Good or bad news? Hard to say isn't it?

(*Slimming Naturally*, November 1979, p. 7)

Example 83

Interest Rates: Gloom for Government

1 The immediate reaction to this week's bank lending figures was exactly what the Government didn't want: fears of yet higher interest rates driving shares down and the pound up.

2 All five main bank groups incurred Bank of England penalties for exceeding their lending limits under the so-called 'corset' system by a total of £419 million.

3 It only served to emphasise that the present system is creaking at the seams. Not even record interest rates of more than 20 per cent for most borrowers are enough to stem demands for loans, largely because they are still cheap when inflation is heading remorselessly for the same level.

(*Now!*, February 1980, p. 67)

Example 84

Fisher Dilemma on Fraud

1 Lloyd's of London chairman Peter Green and almost the entire insurance fraternity have welcomed the recommendations of the Fisher report. A new council to regulate the market and tackle long term problems with the help of three outsiders; the removal of the 20 per cent upper limit on foreign control of member brokers; and the divestment by brokers of their underwriting agency subsidiaries. All have been accepted as both inevitable and just.

2 Only on one issue has a serious note of dissent been raised – fraudulent claims and the duty of a broker. Fisher argues that if a broker is asked to pass on a claim he knows or believes to be fraudulent, it is up to him whether to refuse to press it or not. If he suspects fraud but cannot prove it absolutely, 'he will be in a dilemma to which we see no easy answer.'

3 Several Lloyd's brokers, including Malcolm Pearson, of Savonita fame (otherwise a firm admirer of the report), think that it is not nearly strong enough. A broker suspecting a fraudulent claim should be able to go to the new council, which would then inform other brokers, they feel. Quite right.

(*Sunday Telegraph*, 29 June 1980, p. 18)

Example 85

6½ Prescriptions Each!

1 Over three hundred million prescriptions for drugs were dispensed in 1979, the Social Services department announced in reply to a question in the House of Commons.

2 This was despite the prescription charges rising from 20p to 45p in July 1979.

3 And it works out at an average of six and a half prescriptions for every single person living in Britain.

(*Here's Health*, June 1980, p. 8)

Chapter 8

Evaluating Old and New Solutions

Pre-Evaluation of the Solution

In Chapter 3 we analysed examples in which the four parts of a text's metastructure – Situation, Problem, Solution and Evaluation – were present. What was referred to as 'solution' was seen to be an attempted solution or proposed solution in some examples. It is necessary to make this qualification because inherent in the word 'solution' is the implicit evaluation that it is successful, that is, that it solves the problem. This means that if we describe something simply as a solution we are pre-evaluating it as being a successful means of overcoming the problem.

In many of our examples of the basic metastructure the reader had to wait until he reached the evaluation part after the solution to find out whether the suggested solution actually was a solution (e.g. Example 5). In Example 9, however, we saw how the words *helping to overcome some of these problems* pre-evaluated the Precinct Tree Grid even before it had been introduced and described. Although further evaluation is given later in that example, we still have to recognise the pre-evaluative function of those words. Example 86 is a very clear instance of pre-evaluation. Note the effective combination of active and passive in this example.

Example 86   Pre-Evaluation of a Solution

Working Alone . . .

In the past I have used a portable vice clamped on to a locker lid. That was satisfactory for small jobs, but was not man enough for the heavy equipment used on a sea-going boat. The problem was overcome by bolting a steel engineer's vice to a heavy wooden shelf and resting it on bearers in an inverted position under the engine box lid; in use it can either be turned the right way up in place, or removed and clamped in the cockpit where the heavy shelf helps to keep the vice steady . . .

(*Practical Boat Owner*, June 1979, p. 86)

The general problem the writer needed to solve was to have some means of holding material he was working on. *In the past* his previous solution *was satisfactory for small jobs, but* (note this signal of a problem to come) it *was not man enough* for his present purpose.

As we can already understand this as a problem, the function of *The problem was overcome* is not to classify the previous statement as being a problem; rather it is to pre-evaluate the device about to be described as being an adequate solution to that problem.

The substitute *That* refers to the whole of the first sentence.

The concept of improvement, discussed in Chapter 5, can now also be seen to involve instances of pre-evaluation. The word *improvement* means that a problem or deficiency has been detected in something and that a means has been found to overcome that deficiency; this involves problem recognition, remedial response taken, and evaluation of that response as being an adequate solution to the problem. All these meanings can be seen compressed into the short text of Example 43, where the previous slide bearing pads were not adequate for all required applications, and where a new protective coating was added. The improvement enabled the new pads to be used in environments where the old pads were inadequate. The use of *Improved* in the title of that text provides pre-evaluation of the new protection pads as being a suitable solution to a deficiency in the earlier ones. In the same way, any change for the better that overcomes a deficiency in an 'old' solution carries with it a comparative evaluation, that is, that it is better in some way than the old solution.

The occurrence of pre-evaluation in the introduction of the solution may be all that is necessary for the communication. This was seen in Example 86, where it was not necessary to include a separate part of the description at the end to evaluate the effectiveness of the solution. However, pre-evaluation does not mean that a separate evaluation is not possible. Indeed, the writer may wish to include a brief pre-evaluation in introducing the solution, and then provide further evaluative information after providing details of the solution. This means that there can be a brief evaluation immediately preceding the solution (pre-evaluation), or evaluation of the solution after the details of the solution – or even both.

Two Types of Evaluation of the Solution

The selection of pre-evaluation and/or post-evaluation is a matter of writing choice and the amount of evaluative information to be conveyed. The writer can introduce a possible or attempted solution to a problem and evaluate its effectiveness afterwards. Alternatively, he can intimate the success of the solution as he introduces the solution; and he is also able to provide both pre- and post-evaluation if he desires. We now have to look at the evaluation of solutions more deeply and consider two types of evaluation of the solution.

Two types of evaluation means two types of information that evaluates, rather than a choice as to how the information is reported. That is, we have to recognise two potential groups of evaluative information 'mountains' that may be available for communications; having recognised the two types of information, the writer then has to choose how to communicate it.

One type of evaluative information deals with whether, how, or how well the solution overcomes the problem, and it can be seen as the prime information needed about a solution or proposed or attempted solution. A brief review of some of the earlier examples will show us what is involved with this type of evaluative information.

In Example 5 the evaluation answers the question 'Did ANBESOL stop Peter's teething troubles?' and the evaluations in Example 8 answer the question 'Did the grabbing of the flesh make him admit he had a spare tyre problem?' and 'Did his eating more sensibly reduce his spare tyre?'. These are all positive evaluations, where the attempted solutions actually worked. In Example 11, however, we see that the answer to the evaluative question 'Did the five cats get rid of the rats?' is answered implicitly in the negative, and the evaluative paragraph that follows in that example is easily recognised as another problem. Both 'yes' and 'no' answers to such evaluative questions tell us something about the effectiveness of the attempted solution.

The second type of evaluation about a solution provides detail that does not bear directly on its ability to overcome the stated problem. For example, a new product could be designed to overcome a specific problem, and we would have to be informed whether or not (and perhaps to what extent) it has done that. In addition, the reader may wish to know other evaluative details such as its price, accuracy, appearance, or weight. Example 87 illustrates both types. Note how the subject of the first sentence is split by *is available* to avoid a very long subject with a short verb and complement at the end.

Example 87   Two Types of Evaluation with Several Problems Overcome

1   [1]A combined 15A socket and 20A fused connection unit for air con-ditioners is available that will reduce the time and cost of installation and make maintenance easier. [2]This new MK unit overcomes the problem of room air conditioning installations where, although the

running current is fewer than 13A the large surged current caused by turning the unit on blows the 13A plug fuse.

2 ³Attractively styled, in either a matt chrome or satin brass finish, the Alban unit fits a twin gang socket outlet box eliminating the need for large and unsightly 20A switch fuses. ⁴The product comes with the socket and connection unit pre-wired. ⁵All that is necessary for installation is to connect up with the mains.

(*Production and Industrial Equipment Digest*, March 1979, p. 18; a photograph accompanied the description)

The first sentence introduces the product together with a brief evaluation of the implicit problem that existing socket units take longer to install. That is, this new product is introduced as an improvement on existing products with regard to their respective installation times. The statement that they *make maintenance easier* is also a comparison with existing socket units. The main function of the unit is given in the second sentence with pre-evaluation followed by details of the problem.

The third sentence details the *attractiveness* of the new product – again in comparison with *unsightly* 20A switch fuses, which is a problem with existing products. This new product *eliminates the need* for the unsightly alternative.

In sentence 4 the detail is given that the socket and connection unit are supplied pre-wired, resulting in the easy installation procedure described in the fifth sentence, this procedure is the basis for the earlier statement that the product *will reduce the time and cost of installation*.

Note how the topic of description is mentioned several times in the text: by *This new MK unit, the Alban unit* and then *The product*. There is also a non-finite clause *Attractively styled . . . brass finish* which provides further information, and there is implicit connection in the final sentence with the words *of the unit* being understood after *installation* and *it* being understood after *connect*.

In Example 87 the product's ability to withstand the initial surge of current is an evaluation of how the main problem has now been overcome. Other evaluative details include the maintainability, attractiveness and ease of installation of the new product.

Example 87 is also an illustration of evaluation in two parts: the thinking assessment part, and the basis or evidence on which the assessment is based. The first instance of this occurs with the evaluation of appearance, *Attractively styled*. This is the assessment part of the evaluation of appearance as it is the writer's assessment of the appearance; the evidence for that assessment occurs in the photograph accompanying the original and from this evidence readers can form their own judgement if they like and either agree or disagree with the assessment of appearance offered by the writer.

Another assessment/basis evaluation in Example 87 involves the comparative evaluation that the unit is quicker to install and easier to maintain, as mentioned in the first sentence. The basis for that assessment comes later. We are told that *The unit comes with the socket and connection unit pre-wired* and this, together with the photograph showing the two parts pre-wired, forms the evidence on which the assessment of quicker installation and easier maintenance is based. The reader could have come to the same conclusion himself, but the clear statements of these improvements are very useful to him. Further evidence for the ease of installation is given in the final sentence, from which we can deduce that the installation is very easy indeed.

Evaluation by Comparison

In Chapter 5 we discussed how improvement on a previous solution could be seen as a means of overcoming a deficiency in that solution, and we analysed examples that illustrated improvement by implicit comparison between the old and the new solution. The signals noted in those examples included all those that indicate a change for the better, including the comparative (e.g. *lower* costs) and improvement through change in time (e.g. *Under the old law* . . . *Now*). Also in that chapter we examined how a totally new solution can overcome a deficiency identified in the old or existing solution.

All these instances can now be seen to involve evaluation. Whenever a new solution improves on an existing solution and the writer tells us that, we are given information that tells us how good the new solution is – an evaluation by comparison with the old solution. Thus, if we are told that something new is better in any way when compared with the old or existing system, then that information provides some evaluation of the new solution as well as the old. When a deficiency in an old solution has been identified and the new solution meets the need for the old solution and also overcomes its deficiency, this information provides us with an evaluation of the new solution. Example 88 has many instances of comparative evaluation in it, comparing the new system with the old. The paragraphs contain the following information: a summary of the change, the old system, the new system and major advantage, and finally additional benefits of the new system.

Example 88   Evaluation by Comparison with a Previous System

Reducing Finishing Costs by 70%

1 A new automatic electrostatic powder finishing system (manufactured by Volstatic Coatings) has replaced the two manual wet paint lines at the North London Works of Main Gas Appliances, with the result that the process of coating the side panels for the company's cooker is now faster and much less labour intensive. The purchasing decision was taken after extensive tests at Volstatic's demonstration centre in London, with close co-operation and assistance from the existing paint supplier, International Paint Industrial Coatings.

2   Personnel previously required to operate the manual system were 2 sprayers, 1 loader, 1 unloader, and 1 chargehand, all of whom had to be replaced for a second 8-hour shift each day to maintain a throughput of approximately 1,200 panels.

3   The new automatic powder coating plant, however, employs only 1 loader, 1 unloader, and 1 technician during a single 8-hour shift to achieve the same production. Labour saving is therefore calculated to be around 70%, and also, according to main gas process controller Mr. T. Murray, the powder plant is more convenient to operate, and easier to clean and maintain.

4   Additional benefits are reported through the use of powder instead of paint – namely a more pleasant working environment due to the absence of solvent vapours, a lower reject rate, and a more consistent, durable finish, so essential for consumer 'white goods'.

(*Automation*, January/February 1980, p. 7)

The title provides, in summary form, information about a previous implicit problem – high finishing costs – and their reduction (evaluation) by 70%. In the first sentence we learn that the *new* system that has *replaced* the old one is *faster* and *much less labour intensive*. These are assessments, for which the basis appears in paragraphs 2 and 3. The second sentence tells us that the decision to implement this new system (the new solution) was taken after testing, a matter to be discussed in Chapter 9.

The main advantages of the new system over the old are given by the comparison between paragraphs 2 and 3, the contrast being made clear by *previously* and then *new . . . however*. The main comparison is between the previous manpower requirements and time taken compared with the new figures for these factors, and this is the basis for the earlier assessments of time and labour saving.

The last part of paragraph 3 provides further evaluation of the new system compared with the old by the comparatives *more convenient to operate* and *easier to clean and maintain*. No basis is given for this assessment, and so the source of the assessment is given so that we know who has made it and can thus regard it as skilled and not unsubstantiated opinion.

In the last paragraph *Additional benefits* predicts further positive comparative evaluations to come, and *through the use of powder* (for the new system) *instead of paint* (for the old system) provides the basis for these evaluations. The first of these assessments (*more pleasant working environment*) has further basis in the form of the *absence of solvent vapours*; this was obviously a problem with the old system which has now been avoided. The other assessments are the *lower rejection rate* and the *more consistent, durable finish*, the importance of the latter as an aim being made clear by the statement that it is so essential for consumer 'white goods'.

Recognising Problems and Proposed Solutions

In essence a problem is an adverse evaluation of a situation or solution. We examine something, find it wanting in some respect, and call this a 'problem'. As we saw in Chapters 5 and 6, there are many types of problem and these are produced by many different types of situation and solution. Apart from the more obvious problems such as sitting on rusty chairs, problem identification is an evaluative function which can have basis, assessment, or opinion – or any combination – but before it will be taken seriously by others at least some basis for the assessment that a problem exists is usually necessary.

We now need to re-examine the importance of the recognition of a problem in a text. If a problem is recognised, we expect to learn of an attempted, proposed, or actual solution to that problem. Where, however, no problem is recognised, that is the end of the matter. Example 89 is a complete paragraph taken from the procedures of a juvenile court committee. The language is suitable for juveniles and adults, and the message it presents is unmistakably clear. Note the three uses of *If* to start sentences, and the other use of *if* in the first sentence.

Example 89   Procedure with and without Problem

If the Committee decides to recommend that the charges be dropped, then they may ask the juvenile and the parents if there is any other problem which they want to talk about. If there is a problem, the Committee will try to help. If there is not a problem, the meeting is over.
(Procedures of the Frontenac County Juvenile Court Committee, Kingston, Canada, 1981)

The whole of the message of this paragraph is contingent on the first condition – that the Committee decides to recommend dropping of the charges. In that event, the Committee seeks to determine if there is *any other problem*. The final two sentences tell us of the action to be taken if there is and if there is not a problem.

Evaluations that conclude that something is 'good' do not identify problems; it is only adverse or 'bad' evaluations that do this. Example 90 repays detailed study. It shows various evaluations of an existing law, the adverse ones being problems that initiate proposals for solution.

Example 90   Adverse Evaluations Identifying Problems

Restrictive Trade Practices

1 On March 28 the Government published a Green Paper on Restrictive Trade Practices policy. This forms the second stage in an overall
review of competition policy (see Update July/August 1978 p. iv).
2 The interdepartmental group responsible for the report found that,
although the law governing restrictive trade practices had been effective in removing or preventing a wide range of restrictive agreements,
there had also been a number of criticisms, particularly that the
legislation had in practice proved unduly inflexible.
3 The group also developed the suggestion made in the Green
Paper of May 1978 (Cmnd. 7198) that so-called uncompetitive or anti-
competitive practices – typically devices by one firm for preventing or
impeding other firms from entering its market – should be brought
under more effective control. The Monopolies and Mergers Commission is designed to remedy that weakness.
4 The Restrictive Trade Practices legislation has proved very effective
in relation to goods (it is still too early to assess the effects on services)
in removing restrictive agreements, the report says. Economic assessments indicate that the legislation has achieved its primary objective by
contributing to improved industrial efficiency. The *Resale Prices Acts*
have proved highly effective in ending resale price maintenance, and
the evidence suggests that they have made a contribution to efficiency
in retailing.
5 There are, however, grounds for criticism, it points out. In particular,
the restrictive trade practices legislation is too inflexible, and may
deter or even prevent both insignificant agreements and those that are
significant but desirable. The legislation should accordingly be made
more flexible, and its operation should be simplified. In addition, the
means of enforcement should be strengthened.
6 New provisions for controlling a range of anti-competitive practices
not covered by the Restrictive Trade Practices legislation should be
introduced, the report states. At present such practices – which
normally arise through attempts to abuse a dominant position in a
particular market – can only be examined in the context of a monopoly
reference to the Monopolies and Mergers Commission.
(Professional Administration, July/August 1979, p. 33)

Although the law being reviewed could be taken as a situation worthy
of study in its own right, it is better to regard it as a solution, as its
evaluation is in terms of how well it is *effective in removing or preventing a wide range of restrictive agreements*, that is, how well it overcomes the problem.

The first paragraph places this *review* in the wider perspective of an
overall review, and the summary of the evaluation of the law is given in
the second paragraph. Generally the group concludes that the law is an
effective solution, but it identifies *a number of criticisms* (problems
with the law) and specifies in particular that it is *unduly inflexible*.

In paragraph 3 we learn that an earlier document had identified a problem and had proposed that certain practices *should be brought under more effective control*. This group has developed that proposal, pointing out that the Monopolies and Mergers Commission is *designed to remedy that weakness*. The weakness is the relatively low level of control over those practices.

The fourth paragraph praises the law in many respects. As no problem is identified here, no further action is necessary. The effectiveness of the law on services is not evaluated, and the omission of that information is explained.

The fifth paragraph identifies a problem, *however* signalling the change from 'good' to 'bad' evaluation. The particular problem concentrated on is the one mentioned earlier: the legislation is *too inflexible*. This inflexibility is then seen to *deter* or *prevent* certain agreements, an undesirable effect. The proposed solution is also given in paragraph 5: the law should be made *more flexible*, its operation *simplified* and its enforcement *strengthened*.

The last paragraph identifies a further problem in that the law does *not* cover a certain range of practices. The undesirable situation *At present* is mentioned together with a call for a suitable solution to this problem.

Presenting a Counter-Evaluation

Example 90 (above) is a brief summary of another report, and it highlights the assessment parts of the evaluation rather than the detailed basis for the assessment which can be found in the original report. For purposes of brevity it is necessary to provide the conclusions reached so that readers can understand where the law is thought to be 'good' and where it is thought to be 'bad'. Where it is 'bad', of course, we have a problem, and we will then expect a solution to be suggested. Although the bases for the assessments are not provided, we know where to find the reasoned argument and other evidence that support the conclusions. Should a reader disagree with the conclusions, he would examine the basis for the conclusions, present his own assessment, and provide counter-evidence that favours his own view. In Example 91 the writer chooses to counter an assessment made by someone else. He examines some of the thinking (telling us where to find the whole article if we wish to read all the thinking), and presents his adverse evaluation of the suggestion made. The forcefulness of this article is achieved by the power of its arguments, by the clarity of the structure and by the related paragraphing.

Example 91   A Suggestion Countered by Reasoned Argument

Future Work Concepts

1 A recent article by Lyn Owen in the Sunday Observer attempts to highlight contemporary thinking by sociologists on the future of a society that will only be able to find work for the most highly skilled and creative people.

2 Part of this thinking includes the concept that the young will work, the old will supervise and the middle bracket will do nothing to produce National wealth but will spend their time, according to their skills, in converting houses, building custom cars, reorganising hospitals and landscaping the neighbourhood.

3 According to this concept, once a person has spent several years learning his job and gaining working experience to a point where he is at the peak of his usefulness, he is put out to grass to await the time when he is old enough to take up a supervisory position.

4 What the sociologists fail to realise is that people cannot lay down and pick up a skill with a period of years in between. Such a person would be out of touch with advances in his field, would have lost the habit of regular work and would therefore be unfit to supervise anyone.

5 The escalating unemployable situation is a tremendous social problem but these concepts are not the answer.

(*Original Equipment Manufacturing and Design*, September 1975, p. 3)

The first paragraph introduces the situation and the article the writer is about to discuss, with a hint of the problem being discussed.

The second paragraph explains the solution being advocated, and the third paragraph explains the effect of this solution, the words *put out to grass* indicating the writer's dissatisfaction with the suggestion.

The writer sees a defect in the thinking, and this is highlighted in the fourth paragraph with a point the sociologists *fail* to realise. The basis for this assessment in the first sentence is then given in the second sentence.

In summary, the writer affirms his agreement that the *situation* is a *tremendous social problem but* denies that the ideas suggested are the *answer* to the problem.

The paragraph structure helps the reader to follow the description of the sociologists' thinking and the writer's rebuttal.

The Recognition of Deficiencies in New Solutions

Solutions are not always perfect. In fact, it is far more reasonable to assume that any solution (new or old) is not the final answer, and that someone will eventually be able to improve it or provide a better solution to the problem. Although it is quite common for writers (especially of advertisements) to stress the positive aspects of a solution and leave readers to detect the weaknesses, this is not always the best approach. Apart from the obvious communication and ethical requirements for the writing to present a balanced description of the solution, writers have found that it is often better to recognise deficiencies in new solutions and admit them before opponents point them out. In all honest debate and description, the negative as well as the positive aspects of the solution are communicated to give the reader a balanced view of what is being described or postulated. If something does not do something that readers might assume it might, the writer has a clear duty to state that limitation to prevent any misunderstanding. The writer of Example 92 has gone to great pains to ensure that the reader fully understands the advantages and limitations of the material he is describing.

Example 92   A Clear Example of Honest Evaluation

Timseal architectural timber coating is now available in five shades of brown to suit almost any timber used as an architectural feature; it is also sold in clear for use as an interior finish. The coloured coatings preserve the fresh colour of the wood and act as a water repellent while permitting the passage of water vapour (the illustration above shows how two similar pieces of Baltic redwood react to droplets of water – the Timseal treated piece repelling the water). Timseal does not by itself preserve the timber, but it does help to preserve its beauty, and is compatible with Stanhope Chemicals' wood preservatives. The life of a Timseal coating varies according to circumstances, but applied as recommended over fully-preserved impregnated timber, the makers say it is reasonable to expect a life of four years between coats on a normal exterior site.

(*Building Specification*, April 1976, p. 63; illustration omitted here)

The *now* in the first sentence tells us that the number of shades available has been increased to five to meet a demand (need) for that choice, and the product itself meets the need for the preservation of the colour of wood, and the repelling of water from the wood. The illustration (not reproduced here) shows, by comparison with the same wood when untreated, how the coating repels water, making it form droplets on the surface of the wood rather than sinking into it.

Readers might assume that the coating is a wood preservative, and this misunderstanding is prevented by the inclusion of *Timseal does not by itself preserve the timber* followed, of course, by what it does do. Note the manner in which the writer reports the evaluation of life expectancy. As the life of the product is so dependent on circumstances in which the treated wood is used, perhaps no definite figure can be given as basis. We are given an assessment of life duration which it is *reasonable to expect*. The writer carefully points out that this assessment is that of the makers and is not his; this is signalled by *the makers say*.

Acceptance of a Deficiency in a Solution

In practice, anyone creating or designing something to solve a problem will always seek possible deficiencies in his selected solution. Some such deficiencies may be overcome during refinement of the product, but some may have to be left because it could cost too much or take too long to correct them. This explains why some texts may identify a problem and give no solution. In Example 93 a design change is first evaluated positively and then a problem is detected in it which the designers just have to live with.

Example 93   An Accepted Problem with No Solution

In spite of the enormous depth of the arches, the forces to be resisted in the splice plates at the moment splices proved to be very large. To help reduce these forces, the flanges of the arches were deepened in the region of the splices causing a change in the roof shape which gave quite an acceptable appearance. However this added complications to the detailing, especially adjoining the sloped ends.

(*Specification Associate*, July/August 1974, p. 16)

The problem is that the forces *proved to be very large*. The second sentence introduces the attempted solution which is intended *To help reduce these forces*, the solution *causing* a change in the roof shape which is positively evaluated as *quite an acceptable appearance*. The negative evaluation is signalled by *However, complications* (a problem) being added to the detailing, and so on. This is a problem the designers had to live with, and the paragraph ends here to indicate that we have reached the end of this particular prose structure.

Often solutions are known to be harmful in some way, but are so useful in another that we decide to tolerate them as no better solution is available. All we can then do is minimise the harmful effects; see Example 94. Note the emphasis provided by the separation of *Combs, rollers, driers* from *take their toll*; also note the effect of the comma after *rollers* rather than the use of *and*.

Example 94   Exploiting an Accepted Deficiency

1   **What your hair has to suffer for the sake of beauty!**
2   So much that is vital to keep your hair beautiful is also hard on it.
3   Combs, rollers, driers; they take their toll, but you can't do without them.
4   The least you can do is be really gentle with your hair when you wash it.

5   JOHNSON'S Baby Shampoo is really gentle, really thorough. It leaves your hair beautifully clean and shiny, in the gentlest possible way.

(*Cosmopolitan*, December 1979, p. 130)

The bold title mentions that hair has to *suffer* for the *sake of beauty*, indicating that something has to be tolerated in the process of achieving an aim. This is made clearer in the second sentence: things that are *vital* are also *hard on* the hair.

Specific examples of *Combs, rollers, driers* are given, and we are told that they *take their toll*. The obvious solution to this problem is to reject them as solutions to the aim of achieving beauty and to find another solution; we are told this is not possible, however, as you *can't do without them*. Thus all that can be done is to alleviate the problem as much as possible.

As the problem has to be accepted, being *really gentle with your hair* is recommended as *The least you can do* to alleviate the problem, and the final sentence indicates a means whereby this can be done. Thus the product is seen as a means of alleviating an unsolvable problem that is inherent with a necessary solution to the basic need.

Example 94 is a good example of advertising style. Apart from the short paragraphs and the rhetorical effects of Paragraph 3, we can also recognise the stress applied by the 'cleft' *The least you can do is*. A striking feature of this example is the use of adjectives, especially the repetition of *gentle, gentle* and *gentlest* – a feature stressed for this product. The three uses of the adjective *really* and then the use of *beautifully* would only be found in this genre of prose, and the exclamatory bold heading is also typical of this genre.

Questions
1   What is pre-evaluation? Why is pre-evaluation sometimes better than waiting to provide evaluation at the end of the details of a solution?
2   What are the two basic types of evaluation of a solution? Which is more important and why?
3   Explain how assessment and basis can be applied to both types of evaluation of a solution.
4   How is comparison with other solutions used as a means of evaluating a solution?
5   What is the process whereby an adverse evaluation of a situation or existing solution is reported as a problem to be solved? How do 'good' evaluations fit into this?
6   Explain the need for clear basis when establishing a point of view and/or countering another's point of view. How does being given the basis for an assessment help the reader?

Examples for Exercises
Here are a few hints on the structures to be found in the examples that follow.

95 *Polyurethane for the Piste* Contains a variety of interesting evaluations. Note the style, and the use of the imperative.
96 *Easier Rider* Pre-evaluation and post-evaluation with modification of an unsatisfactory solution. The title is interesting.
97 *Teeth and Smiles* Problem with solution leads to modification.

Example 95   Polyurethane for the Piste

1   [1]Whether you risk broken limbs on the novice slopes or fancy a little slalom on the piste there's one après-ski you'll not be able to avoid – cold, aching numbed feet. [2]From ancient leather boots to today's plastics equivalent nothing could assuage that below the ankle burden – that is until the advent of 'foamies'. [3]Now fiercely challenging the Alpine strongholds of ski-boot conservatism, 'foamies' are the latest in custom sports footwear. [4]Take a sturdy plastic or magnesium alloy boot shell, insert into it the prospective customer's foot and inject in a dose of polyurethane or silicone rubber foam compound. [5]The result is a warm, springy but firm inner moulding that conforms to every corn, bunion and hammer toe of the user's foot.
2   [6]The boots are described by one prosaic advocate as 'power-steering', an expression of the strong sense of control they give to even the ropiest skier. [7]Marketed by over a dozen American companies, 'foamies' have achieved a healthy ten per cent market share in the first session of operation. [8]There are drawbacks to the development however – users are advised to wear the same pair of socks for every outing as even small size differences within the boot can cause suffering. [9]And for those whose feet swell during long, slippered snowbound evenings the mornings could bring cramped, cold comfort.

(*Design*, April 1971, p. 80)

Example 96   Easier Rider

I had a problem moving a heavy electric cooker, for cleaning, across an uneven quarry tiled floor. Using 'easy rider', I found that the feet of the cooker wandered off quite dangerously. I overcame this by rivetting plastic furniture rests to the tops of the riders. The cooker feet now fit firmly into these making the moving job less hazardous.

(*Practical Householder*, May 1980, p. 14)

Example 97   Teeth and Smiles

Having to wear braces to strengthen teeth can be damaging to one's vanity so Dr. Craven Kurz, an American dentist, has finally come up with the bright idea of putting braces inside the teeth. They're kept in place by a strong acrylic resin and the first few patients, including an actress, are reported to be delighted. Only drawback is that they cost about £2,000.

(*Honey*, March 1980, p. 12)

Chapter 9

Comparative Evaluation and Test Procedures

Evaluative Comments Preceding Revision

The concept of evaluation is one that is fundamental to all organised thought processes, and this book does scant justice to the full meanings and uses of evaluation in texts. The ability of a person to judge and compare intelligently and knowledgeably should be the most important aspect of any educational programme, and what you learn here provides only a basic introduction to this very important subject.

It is only when something is actually created (in real life, not on the drawing board) and used as it is intended to be used that the writer will be in a firm position to report whether or not it works. However, that is simply not practical. We cannot make every crazy idea a reality and thoroughly test it before rejecting it. Nothing would ever be done. So instead there has to be a means by which there is meaningful partial evaluation and reporting in texts at quite early stages of the creation process.

For new or changed laws and procedures, the usual way to proceed is for the new creation to be presented in the form of a proposal or 'discussion paper' or 'draft suggestion' or 'consultative document'. Example 98 is a report in which two such consultative documents are introduced with a clear invitation for evaluative comments on the proposals as part of the evaluation and refinement procedure. Note the punctuation in the second paragraph.

Example 98   Invitations To Provide Evaluative Comments

Patients First

1   Following the report of the Royal Commission on the National Health Service, the Government has published a Consultative Paper on its structure and management in England and Wales, entitled 'Patients First'.

2   Comments on its proposals are requested by April 30, 1980. Briefly, the paper proposes the replacement of area health authorities in multi-

district areas by district health authorities following a review by the Regional Health Authority; the strengthening of hospital and community services management; the continuance of Family Practitioner Committees, whilst the future of Community Health Councils is in doubt; and the simplification of the professional advisory machinery. In Wales, it is proposed that area health authorities should eliminate the district structure. It is not proposed to hold a special enquiry into the health service in London. All structural changes should be completed by the end of 1983. The new districts would have a membership of 20 and a management team of the same composition as the existing area management teams.

3 Comments are also requested by April 30, 1980 on the Government's consultative document *Structure and Management of the NHS in Scotland*.

4 It is proposed to abolish the district tier, the functions of which would generally be transferred to sector and unit level, rather than to area level. Health Councils are under scrutiny.

(Professional Administration, March 1980, p. 36)

The background to the consultative papers is very short, clearly indicating that readers will already know that the problems have been thoroughly identified in a recent report. The consultative paper 'Patients First' is a proposed solution to the problems, and no doubt it will also contain ample evaluative discussion as to the expected effectiveness of the proposals. Note the many occasions when *proposal* and variants are used in the text.

The invitation has a deadline of 30 April, and this is followed by details, given briefly, of the important features of the proposals – enough to give a clear summary. The third paragraph tells us what is *not* proposed, a denial of an expected proposal. The last two paragraphs include a request for comments on another consultative document, again with brief summary details of the proposals. The final sentence tells us that a related situation is *under scrutiny*; should problems become apparent, no doubt a further consultative document will be produced with proposed solutions to them.

Asking for Constructive Criticism

The need for views to be heard, and for everyone to have an opportunity to express their views, can become very important when public projects such as new airports or proposed large sewage or water development projects are planned. The right of people to make their views known is made part of the legislation protecting the rights of individuals where projects might harm their interests, and 'public inquiries' on various topics are frequently in the news as these provide a forum for public criticism and debate. Example 99 illustrates a typical call for people to come to a meeting to hear about new proposals and to express their views on them. Note how the reported speech is made part of the text, a technique used extensively in many quite informal reports.

Example 99   A Meeting To Learn about Proposals and Express Views

Your Chance to Speak

1 To facilitate making known opinions in industry on the new accident reporting proposals, the Senior Executive Briefings Division of the British Safety Council will hold a Consultative Workshop on the Training Ship 'St. Katharine' in London on Thursday, May 17.
2 Speakers and reporters will include safety professionals well known to those attending BSC training courses – as well as Mrs. G. Berenzweig of the Health and Safety Executive Policy Division.
3 'We recognise the need for stronger consultation with the people who will be expected to implement the new law, and the workshop will brief you on the proposals and collect your comments for presentation to the Health and Safety Executive. But come prepared to work because this promises to be a VERY full day', advises BSC Director-General Tye.

(*Safety*, April 1979, p. 32)

The title indicates an opportunity to express views on something, and this is made more specific in the first paragraph. The meeting is for *making known opinions* on some new *proposals*. The second paragraph tells us that experts will be available to provide information as a basis for people to assess the new proposals and then to express their views.

The third paragraph stresses the importance of obtaining the views of those who will implement the new law, and points out that details of the proposals will be made available.

The purpose of the meeting should not just be to try to convince people that the proposals are sound, but more to obtain skilled assessments which will form the basis of improvements to the proposals before they actually become law. That is, the Safety Council are seeking constructive comments and criticism which will enable safety officials and politicians to improve the proposals; such criticism is different from destructive criticism, which is intended purely to block proposals.

Preliminary and Final Testing

The pharmaceutical industry and related medical practice has particularly grave problems when it comes to evaluating the effectiveness (and possible side-effects) of drugs. Because there can be no full evaluation of new drugs until they are actually tried out on humans in a normal environment, and also because such tests can be dangerous, many drug evaluation procedures use animals as 'guinea pigs' to try out the product. After exhaustive tests to determine whether there are likely to be any serious side-effects, the research then turns to trials on human 'guinea pigs' and finally to selective testing in certain areas. This helps to explain the structure of Example 100, which deals with a case where a new product has already been tested but further tests are needed before meaningful conclusions can be drawn.

Example 100   Evaluation Procedure Involving Animals

Chinese Pillpuzzle

1   One spin-off from the new friendliness between America and China is investigation into a new male birth pill, claimed by Chinese scientists to be virtually 100 percent effective.
2   The pill, a chemical called gossypol which is made from cotton seed, is to be tested on animals by the US Rockefeller Foundation and the Population Council. Chinese doctors say that they have tested the substance at very low doses in 3,000 men over the past four years, and that it is 99.8 percent effective. There are said to be no adverse effects on sexual performance or on fertility, and other side-effects are few.
3   However, one American pharmacologist, on a recent study tour of China, discovered stomach upsets and vomiting in some cases. Also gossypol is in some respects an unknown quantity – at high doses it is well-established as a poisonous chemical though the Chinese may have purified the chemical to minimise such problems. How the drug works is not clear.
4   The director of the US centre where gossypol is to be tested says the Chinese pill is 'interesting and potentially important but at this stage it is premature to draw conclusions'.

(*Cosmopolitan*, April 1979, p. 18)

The situation and the problem the new male birth pill is designed to overcome are so obvious that there is no need to state them – compare this with Example 23. Thus the first paragraph is the new solution together with an evaluation by Chinese scientists. The second sentence tells us what the pill is called, what it is made from, that it is to be *tested* on animals, and the testing agency.

Positive evaluation comes in paragraph 2 in terms of the test carried out together with results (finding or assessment based on the test). The assessments *no adverse effects* and *other side effects are few* are further positive assessments based on the test data.

Negative evaluations are provided in paragraph 3 after the signal

However. The discovery of *stomach upsets* and *vomiting* identifies problems with the new pill. Its poisonous nature is identified as a potential problem, but this is partly countered in that the Chinese *may have purified* (a solution) the chemical. That the pill is an unknown quantity and that *How the drug works is not clear* are problems because the effects cannot be predicted by theoretical analysis; they require empirical tests.

The current assessment is given in the final paragraph. The basis is all the data available to the director, including the tests and findings of the Chinese researchers. He feels that there is insufficient evidence at this stage for meaningful conclusions to be drawn, and therefore further tests are needed. This shows the level of integrity we expect of researchers and of texts that explain their work.

The next stage in the testing of pharmaceutical products is to try out the product on a selected small group of people. Once there is clear scientific evidence that there are no dangerous side-effects, trials of the drug can be made in the environment in which the drug will ultimately be used. This same procedure is used in marketing a new product. This understanding helps us to recognise the structures of many texts.

Theoretical and Practical Evaluation

In Example 101 researchers did not know how the new pill worked and so they could not work out theoretically what the likely effects would be and then test these deductions in practical tests. Theoretical evaluation can be of great importance. A design or hypothesis is examined theoretically (often mathematically) to determine whether it will meet the requirements specified for it. The stresses in all members of a new bridge, for example, are calculated under different assumed load and wind conditions before a design is accepted, as those working on a project need to know that the design will 'work' in practice before they complete it in detail. The same applies to a scientific discovery: the workers assess the likely success of the discovery before proceeding with expensive and often time-consuming tests in the environment in which the discovery will be applied if it proves successful. Our knowledge of theoretical and practical testing helps us to recognise the structures of Example 101.

Example 101   A Solution Considered Theoretically, and Practical Testing

Bio-War in the Greenhouse

1 Botanists may at last have developed an effective way of eradicating one of the most persistent pests in glasshouses, *Myzus persicae*, the peach potato aphis.

2 *Myzus persicae* is an aphis, or plant bug, that attacks a variety of crops, and is especially hard to control in commercial chrysanthemum glasshouses. When sparsely scattered over the plants, it does little damage, but in the warm humid glasshouse, it multiplies rapidly, and attacks the flowers, making them unsaleable. Pesticides are only partially effective, because the aphids congregate on the underside of the tightly packed young leaves where the spray cannot reach.

3   R. A. Hall and H. D. Burgess of the Glasshouse Crops Research Institute, at Littlehampton, came across *Verticillium lecanii*, a tropical fungus related to a plant pathogen that causes wilt in tomato plants. *V. lecanii* is known to attack tropical insects, so Hall and Burgess cultivated it in a nutrient solution and sprayed the fungal spores on to glasshouse chrysanthemums most susceptible to aphis attack (*Annals of Applied Biology*, vol. 93, p. 235). Two factors favoured the fungus. One is the high temperature and humidity of the glasshouse; the other is that *Myzus* is a restless bug. Even when infected, it wanders among its siblings spreading disease, so that even those clustered under the leaf rosettes are killed.

4   Results have been spectacular. In some cases the aphids have disappeared completely, though success with a couple of minor insect pests has been uneven. But Hall and Burgess hope that the tests they are now doing will confirm their results, and succeed even with the minor pests. Chrysanthemum growers will be watching their progress with interest.

(*New Scientist*, 13 March 1980, p. 832)

We quickly learn of the situation with *Greenhouse* and *Botanists*, and *Bio-War* indicates a problem and attempted solution within this situation. The first paragraph is an introductory summary with a pre-evaluation and problem, as is made clear by *an effective way of eradicating*.

The second paragraph presents the problem in greater detail, with a more specific situation given in the first sentence. The problem is not too bad when the pests are sparsely scattered *but* it is bad in the warm glasshouse. The seriousness of the problem is made progressively clear by *it multiplies rapidly*, then *attacks the flowers*, finally making them *unsaleable*. (The same structure can be seen in Example 33.) The obvious solution has to be mentioned and rejected (with basis for the rejection) as pesticides are the obvious solution to this problem. The basis for rejection of pesticides is later seen to be overcome by the new solution.

Some details of the fungus as an enemy of the aphis are given, and the possible success of this technique is considered theoretically in terms of the two factors favouring the fungus. The first is the humidity and temperature, and the second is the mobility of the aphis; it is this mobility that causes their deaths even when they cluster under young leaves, and this solution is therefore seen to overcome the deficiency in the use of pesticides mentioned earlier.

Details of the practical tests are then given and are assessed as *spectacular* with basis for that assessment following. Further tests are under way in an attempt to confirm the positive evaluation. Note the evaluation of the project as *interesting* from the point of view of chrysanthemum growers.

Comparison of Solutions (Value Judgement)

In Chapter 8 the concept of 'value judgement' was introduced in terms of comparative evaluations of possible solutions. These comparative evaluations of different competing solutions form the basis for the decision to continue with one selected solution. The decision-maker has to have comparative data as a basis for the assessments and decision, and this often involves the running of different stages of comparative tests for the competing solutions – the same sort of procedure used for selection at beauty contests. Example 102 follows this structure. This is a brief summary of a complex procedure and it contains many interesting features.

Example 102   A Series of Tests for Comparative Evaluation

Improved Insulation for Cryogenic Power-Transmission Cables

1 [1]Stemming from extensive investigations carried out in the U.S.A. by the General Electric Research and Development Center, an improved electrical insulation is believed to represent a significant advance in the development of cryogenic electrical power-transmission cables. [2]In fact this insulation, which is expected to withstand well over 500 kV at temperatures around $-320°F$, promises to become one of the key building blocks in one type of high-capacity underground transmission system of the future. [3]At the same time it will meet the burgeoning power-transmission needs in an environmentally and economically acceptable manner. [4]In this regard it is estimated that a cryogenic cable system could have the capacity to transmit up to 5000 MVA in a single circuit; by contrast a 500-MVA rating is considered high for the conventional oil-filled underground cables now serving metropolitan areas.

2 [5]The new insulating material – a modified cellulose paper tape – is the most promising of more than 200 samples of electrical insulation investigated, a selected few of which were subjected to extra-high voltages to determine their breakdown strength. [6]For this purpose, they were immersed in a specially constructed high-voltage test facility, based on three pressure vessels 20ft in height and filled with liquid nitrogen. [7]To evaluate the new material, sections of cryogenic cable 40 ft in length have been wrapped with this insulation and are currently undergoing sustained testing.

(*Engineers' Digest*, April 1976, p. 16; from *Iron Age*, 26 January 1976, p. 30)

The title provides the situation of insulation for very low temperature power-transmission cables together with an implicit problem and evaluated intimation of a solution in the word *Improved*. The situation is made more specific in the first sentence, which also includes further evaluation in the form *represent a significant advance*. The use of *is believed to* signals that the evaluation is not yet definite and that the writer is reporting the extent of current knowledge.

The assessment in the first sentence is provided with some basis in the second sentence, where *is expected to* and *promises* again signal the 'hypothetical' nature of the evidence given. The third sentence, which stresses that it will *meet . . . needs* in an *acceptable* way, provides an evaluation of the solution to meet the needs and also an evaluation of other important features of the solution. The assessment in the third sentence that the new insulation *will meet the burgeoning power-transmission needs* is given clear support (basis) in the fourth sentence. First we learn that it is *estimated* (again hypothetical) that it could enable up to 5,000 MVA to be transmitted in a single circuit; then, to provide the means for the reader to use this figure as a basis for his own assessment, we are given the *considered high* value for conventional cables as a contrast.

The second paragraph tells us of the testing procedures used. First we learn that there were more than 200 samples from which were *selected a few*, obviously on the basis of a comparative assessment of the 200 samples. These selected few *were subjected to extra-high voltages to determine their breakdown strength*. From this we can tell that the insulation being described here was judged to be the best. The seventh sentence informs us that the selected insulation, which shows such promise from the tests so far, is *currently undergoing sustained testing*. The idea of this testing is to provide a firm evaluation of its breakdown characteristics over a long period of time, thus turning the present 'hypothetical' evaluation into a firm 'real' one.

Description of comparative evaluation is often very important. There is rarely an obvious single solution to a problem, and the possible solutions need to be described and analysed in some detail before the decision to select one of them is reported. To help readers to make a meaningful comparison between the rival solutions, their pros and cons may have to be described, and this may involve discussion of related testing.

Weighing the pros and cons of competing solutions is a very common structure in texts. Any choice involves the weighing of the advantages and disadvantages of the alternatives, and texts reflect this need. In Example 23 we analysed only one alternative, looking at its main features, its good points and its bad points. However, the series of articles from which that was taken dealt with all common alternatives, again giving their pros and cons. This enabled readers to assess and compare the contraceptive alternatives available to them and to decide which method or methods to use.

Testing as a Basis for Decision and Implementation

When we buy clothes, we usually try them on first, and we would always 'test-drive' a car before buying it. Purchasers of major equipment also want to be certain before buying. They need to know whether the product they are interested in is suitable for their needs, and the only way to be sure about this is to test the equipment in their own environment. Example 103 is a typical short report of such testing; it relies on the well-known euphemism 'helping the police with their inquiries' for the double meaning of the title.

Example 103   A System Being Tested

CADC Helps Police with their Inquiries

1   A much more flexible alternative to the conventional Identikit and Photofit methods used by the police to build up a picture of a suspect's face has been developed by the Computer Aided Design Centre on behalf of the Police Scientific Development Branch. It could have great export potential.

2   The system involves a colour graphics terminal linked to a computer in which a databank of standard facial features has been stored. The features can be selected to build up a composite face on the display that fits the description of the witness.

3   The biggest advantage of the CADC system over conventional methods is that the policeman operating the display can modify individual facial features on the screen to fit more closely a witness' description. The tonal range of the face colouration can also be modified.

4   PSDB personnel are currently evaluating the system at CADC in Cambridge where the software is being run on a Prime 300 minicomputer. The fact that it is written in Fortran means that it could be used with most kinds of computer, including most police systems.

5   The CADC Gino graphics package, which is also written in Fortran, is run on systems all over the world.

6   The police system is currently being tested using the CADC advanced graphics display terminal, otherwise known as Bugstore.

(*Computer Weekly*, 30 November 1978, p. 64)

The first paragraph pre-evaluates the new system as *A much more flexible alternative*, and this is later followed by the evaluative sentence assessing the *great export potential*. No details of the situation or problem are given, as these are clearly understood by the readers. The second paragraph provides detail of the system, and the third evaluates the system by comparison with conventional methods.

The fourth paragraph tells us in the first sentence that the police are *currently evaluating* the system, and the second sentence provides details of compatibility with other police systems. The last two paragraphs provide details of the CADC display package on which the new system is being tested. Presumably if the tests are a success the police will purchase the system and integrate it into their computer network.

Once a solution has been tested and proved to be adequate, the obvious next step is to implement the solution and then evaluate how well it works in practice. An example of evaluation after a law has been implemented is given in Example 90, where problems were detected in an implemented solution. In Example 104 tests have shown that the solution is effective under certain circumstances, and the question of implementing the solution is answered in the final paragraph.

Example 104   Implementing a Tested and Proved Solution

Hats Save Heat

[1]Newborn babies can lose heat very quickly and become hypothermic and it is well known that too great a heat loss in the first few moments of life can cause tiny newborn babies to die. [2]Doctors from the London Hospital Medical College are now recommending that all newborn babies should be given a heat-saving hat made from Gamgee (vernaid gauze and cotton tissue). [3]Tests showed that wearing such hats caused a big reduction in heat lost although the temperature of the room the babies were born in and length of time they remained unwrapped were also important. [4]For most strong, healthy babies a small amount of cooling will do little harm, but in cases where prematurity or other factors weaken the child, heat saving can be vital. [5]Hospitals may soon be supplied with these hats, but mothers having their babies at home and wishing to make a hat can get Gamgee from their local chemist.
(*Family Circle*, July 1980, p. 25; from *British Medical Journal*, February 1979, p. 25)

The situation is *Newborn babies* and the recognised problem is that *they can lose heat very quickly and become hypothermic*. The potential seriousness of this problem is made clear in the same sentence, the result of the heat loss possibly causing *tiny newborn babies to die*. The recommendation is a request for implementation of a solution, and the solution is then specified. The use of *heat-saving* indicates that the solution is intended as a means of overcoming the problem just defined.

Assessment of *Tests* is given as *caused a big reduction in heat lost*, with no basis for that assessment being offered. It is conceded that room temperature and other clothing are also important factors affecting heat loss, the Gamgee being only a partial solution to be used sensibly with other means of keeping the babies warm. A further concession is made that small heat loss is not too important for strong healthy babies, *but* this is seen in contrast with the conclusion that for weak babies *heat saving* can be *vital*. For such babies, the Gamgee is seen as a useful and perhaps important device that could save a weak baby's life.

Implementation is discussed in the final sentence in two forms: the hats *may* (hypothetical) soon be supplied to hospitals, and future mothers can make a hat for themselves after buying Gamgee from a local chemist (drugstore).

Questions

1   What is the need for texts that are 'consultative documents'?
2   What are constructive and destructive criticisms?
3   What is the importance of signals of hypotheticality (which indicate lack of knowledge) for texts explaining preliminary tests or the testing of new drugs on animals?
4   What is the difference between theoretical and practical testing? What are typical signals in the text that tell the reader which is which?
5   What, in general terms, is the procedure for value judgement of competing solutions and the selection of the best? How do texts reflect this?
6   What is meant by the structure of 'weighing the pros and cons' with respect to comparative evaluation?

Examples for Exercises

Here are hints on the structures to be found in the examples that follow.

105   *Biofeedback Stops Reynaud's Attack*   Initial assessment supported by tests of two techniques.
106   *'Hazfile' Computer Launch*   The new scheme has a purpose which complements the purpose of an existing system. It is run as a pilot project before a final decision is made.

Example 105   Biofeedback Stops Reynaud's Attack

1   Of 20 patients in an American project, 19 could stop a Reynaud's attack after being taught relaxation techniques using biofeedback.
2   The disease is a disorder of small arteries which results in sudden attacks of coldness, usually in the hands or feet. The attacks are due to a reduction in blood flow caused by a spasm of the arteries.
3   In one technique patients had their skin temperature changes monitored by a light staying on when their temperature rose and going off when it dropped.
4   The second technique involved a tape recording that told patients to relax and imagine they were lying on a beach in the sun.
5   The biofeedback techniques were practised for an hour, three times a week, for a month.
6   After three months, 19 of the 20 patients were able to raise their

temperature at least 2.8°C above baseline. They could thus prevent a Reynaud's attack, even when they were exposed in a cold room.

(*Here's Health*, April 1980, p. 8)

Example 106   'Hazfile' Computer Launch

1   The 'Hazfile' scheme to provide computer-stored information to fire brigades about chemicals involved in incidents was launched in the New Year by AERE Harwell's Chemical Emergency Centre.
2   The Hazfile scheme will complement Chemsafe, the existing manned telephone operation at Harwell to identify and advise on chemicals.
3   Initially to be run as a one-year pilot project with fifteen selected fire brigades in England, Scotland and Wales, Hazfile provides rapid retrieval of hazard information and manufacturers' identity by on-line telephone access.
4   The information is to be stored in a data bank by the BOC-datasolve computer bureau — covering over 10,000 substances identified by chemical and trade names.

(*Safety*, February 1979, p. 2)

Appendix: A Guide to the Analysis of Texts

No 'Method' Offered

This book is not intended to offer a rigorous and infallible model or analytical method by which you can mechanically analyse the structure of texts in everyday English use. Instead its purpose is to provide you with an understanding of the basic structures, their complications and related signalling words, which you can then apply intelligently to such texts. The aim is to provide a meaningful education in the subject rather than attempting to instil any particular methodology for textual analysis.

We usually cannot lay a crude template of 'Situation–Problem–Solution–Evaluation' over a text and expect the parts to become readily apparent. Actual examples of language present an infinite variety of information organisation and signalling, and the only way we can expect to analyse them is to understand the underlying principles of prose structures and to apply these to each new text we are faced with. Throughout the book many typical structures (e.g. Problem–Solution, Situation–Evaluation) have been identified and the examples analysed can be seen to some extent as models of these typical structures. But each text will be different in some way, and you should not think that simple recognition of the basic structure of a text will yield an adequate analysis.

The analyses presented throughout the book are not intended to be complete although they do describe the major prose structures and signalling together with any interesting stylistic or grammatical features of the examples. In reading the analyses, you should first read the example at least twice and note the heading provided for it to indicate its main educational point for this book. Ideally you could write out your own analysis of the text before reading the analysis offered. Then read the analysis carefully, relating it to the example, and noting how specific words and groups of words are highlighted in the analysis and made an integral part of the analysis. These words should be seen as key elements of the example as they tell readers what types of information are being presented and how this information is interrelated.

A Series of Steps (for students)

Here is a very general series of steps which should help you to analyse examples of everyday English use. You should not regard these steps as being a substitute for detailed study of the structure and words of the text, or as an infallible method which must result in an adequate analysis. Instead you must be guided by your own developing understanding of language structure and signalling, and it is best to treat these steps as a detailed checklist that helps you to apply that understanding. If a specific test/examination question has been set you must, of course, answer all the parts asked for, and you should read the question very carefully and ensure you provide the information requested.

(1) Read the text through carefully at least once.

(2) Read it through again, underlining or circling words or groups of words that signal or control information structures in the text.

(3) Try to determine the overall structure of the text – whether it is a complete success story in four-part structure, a failed or otherwise 'incomplete' account, or a structure such as 'Situation–Evaluation' or 'Problem–Solution'. For 'incomplete' structures, try to understand why certain parts of the four-part metastructure have not been included (e.g. readers know it, or it will be obvious to readers, or the information is not available).

(4) Determine the informational role of the title of the example and any headings it has, and look for introductory summaries in the title and/or the first paragraph. Also look for other condensed structures (perhaps for minor 'Problem–Solution' structures) throughout the text.

(5) Examine the text again to see if there are perhaps two or more problems, or two or more solutions, or conflicting evaluations.

(6) Try to identify any deficiencies with old solutions as the problem being dealt with.

(7) Study the 'Solution' carefully to determine whether it is actually a solution or is perhaps a proposed solution or an attempted solution which has yet to be evaluated or implemented. Also determine whether implementation has or has not taken place and exactly what is being evaluated.

(8) Now describe the text, using important structure words to highlight your analysis and trying to explain as fully as possible the structures of information in the text and the way they are signalled and integrated.

(9) Read the text as a whole once again, seeking to refine your analysis. Look for such things as assessment and basis for evaluation (they may not occur next to each other in the text), try to classify the type of problem communicated, look out for the causes of problems and whether the solution is aimed at the initiating or resulting problem, and determine whether the solution is evaluated as a solution or for other features – or both. Such detailed analysis will sharpen your awareness of language structure in a way that nothing else will.

(10) Decide whether a structural diagram will help your description; if so, draw one and label it as completely as you can.

(11) Then re-examine the text for its style: the suitability of word choice, paragraphing, any informalities, grammatical structures and coherence devices for the genre of the text. Comment accordingly, again citing specific features of style in the text that have led you to your conclusions.

(12) Note any interesting feature of coherence, word choice, sentence structure, punctuation, and so on, that you observe in the text and that will help readers of your analysis to learn from the study of the text and your analysis.

(13) Finally read over your analysis carefully to ensure that it is well written: that it is clear and concise; that it does not contain errors of spelling or punctuation; and that it is stylistically suitable for a formal communication to your teacher.

Suggestions for Classroom Analysis (for teachers)

Analysis of actual English use can be and should be fun for the student. The examples themselves are usually interesting, and students soon find out that they learn much about life in general from the examples they analyse. The obvious classroom technique for analysis, of course, is simply to give students an example and ask them to analyse it in accordance with the analyses offered in this book; but there are other techniques that also prove useful and rewarding for both teacher and student if class sizes permit.

(1) Ask a student, after he has had adequate time to think about it, to present an analysis orally to the rest of the class, and then ask for comments/criticisms of the analysis from the rest of the class. This is an ideal starting point for the analysis of complex examples, and it is a sound vehicle for helping students to make clear presentations in class.

(2) Arrange students in groups to work together and present a written group analysis; alternatively, have each group nominate a leader to present his group's analysis for comments by other members of the class.

(3) Have the students write a rough analysis to be checked by you. They can then write a good version of the analysis, and produce something they can be proud of.

(4) Have the students work in pairs or small groups, each student preparing a written analysis and colleagues commenting on it with a view to improving it. The teacher's role becomes one of arbitrating the inevitable, and highly desirable, discussions and differences of opinion. As long as the teacher knows the texts well, it is quite possible to have different groups working at their own pace on different examples.

(5) Encourage the students to bring in their own examples for analysis in the class, first allowing the teacher to provide enough copies of the text for the whole class.

(6) Arrange projects where different students and groups collect their own examples of a specified type of structure and present the collection together with its analysis.

(7) Get the students to ask the teacher about difficulties they are having analysing a text, each student working on an individual basis. Only when they feel they thoroughly understand the text should they be encouraged to write the analysis.

It is really quite surprising how interested students can become about structures and signalling in texts when they are given the opportunity to study the subject free from the usual inhibitions created by traditional rules of 'effective' writing.

Test Questions (for examiners)

Although simply giving students texts and asking them to analyse them in accordance with the analyses in this book will work, it is far more satisfactory if specific test/examination questions are set for each text. Here is an example of the sort of question that would be suitable for Example 33.

Explain the information structure of this example, paying particular attention to the use of summaries in the text. Clearly identify all words in the text that help you to identify the types of information in the text. Describe fully the interconnected chain of logic related to identification of the problem, explain the full meanings of the two structures dominated by *It is well known that . . . However* and *It is true that . . . but*, and discuss the significance of the final sentence in relation to the first. Finally identify which parts are reported as definite and which parts are reported as hypothetical, specifying all signals of hypotheticality.

Such an analysis could take most students 50–60 minutes to do well.

INDEXES

The special indexes provided here will enable you to study various aspects of prose structure and coherence through examining structures or words in the contexts of the examples. All entries except the conventional subject index at the end refer to example numbers and paragraph numbers where relevant; thus **91/5** refers to the fifth paragraph of Example 91. When two or more occurrences appear in one example or paragraph, this is indicated in brackets; thus **45/2(2)** under the word *only* means that there are two instances of the word *only* in the second paragraph of Example 45. In addition **Ab** means abstract and **T** means title.

Index A	Information Structures	*page* 142
Index B	Types of Problem	143
Index C	Words of Coherence	145
Index D	Signals of Logic	146
Index E	Subordinators	147
Index F	Hypotheticals	148
Index G	Prefixes and Suffixes	149
Index H	Time Indicators	150
Index I	Informal Style Indications	151
Index J	Key Words	152
Index K	Subject Index	159

Index A: Information Structures

This index lists the occurrences of different types of information structure in the examples. The entries should be regarded only as an informative basis for further study and not as a definitive analysis.

Situation–Problem–Solution–Evaluation 4, 5, 6, 7, 8, 9, 10, 13(2), 14, 15, 31, 33, 38, 39, 40, 41, 42, 55, 61/2, 61/3, 64, 72, 86, 87, 94, 95, 96, 101

Problem–Solution–Evaluation 30, 31/1, 34, 65, 71, 73, 90, 93, 97

Problem–Solution 24, 25, 27, 34/3, 37, 93, 97

Solution–Problem 1, 26, 32/1, 36, 66, 67

Situation–Problem–Solution 16, 17, 28, 29, 49, 50, 51, 58(4), 59, 60, 62, 98

Solution–Evaluation 21, 22, 23, 92, 100, 102, 103, 104, 105, 106

Situation–Problem 56, 57/2, 63, 68, 83

Situation–Evaluation 69, 70, 74, 75, 76, 77, 78, 79/1, 79/2, 80, 80/2, 81, 82, 84, 85, 89, 91

Solution 19, 20

Pre-evaluation 9, 39, 41, 86, 96

Condensed structures 13T, 18/1, 18/3, 31/1, 32/1, 33T, 33/1, 35/1, 37, 41/3(2), 43, 50/1, 55, 57/1, 59/1, 61/1, 87/1, 101/1, 106/1

Comparison/improvement or deficiency with existing or obvious solution 1, 41/1, 42, 43, 44, 45, 46, 47, 48, 52, 53, 54, 86, 88, 96, 101/2

Implementation 15, 104, 106

Accepted deficiency in solution 93, 94, 97

Failure of attempted solution 11, 12, 57/1

Seeking evaluation 98, 99

Index B: Types of Problem

This index provides a rough classification of many of the problems identified in the examples. There is some overlapping of the categories, and this index should be regarded more as a basis for study and discussion than as a definitive listing.

Key words are given along with the example number and paragraph to enable you to find each entry quickly, and implicit problems are shown by an asterisk.

Not Good Enough 9/4 improve irrigation*; 10/1 increase operating temperature*; 10/1 higher efficiency* and higher fuel consumption*; 13/1 more efficiently*; 23/6 very, very unreliable; 30/1 inadequately catered for; 37 dentures let them down; 42/2 unlikely to turn heads; 43 increased protection*; 44 unsuitable for goods of a hygroscopic nature; 44 vulnerable to moisture and gas; 46/1 no longer meets new regulations*; 65/2 callers seem to be whispering; 71/1 lack of vitality*; 73 inadequate life and colour rendition*; 74 slow; 74 not notably suitable voice; 74 frigidity; 79/2 in the doldrums; 81T too lax; 86 not man enough; 87/1 reduce time and cost of installation and make maintenance easier*; 88/1 faster and less labour intensive*; 90/2 unduly inflexible; 96 feet wandered off dangerously; 101/2 unsaleable

Too Many, Too Much 11/2 overrun by cats; 11/2 overrun by rats; 12/1 massive rodent population; 13/3 cost $5; 13/4 24 hours to get through; 53 what a price!; 56/2 too expensive; 56/2 too valuable to stay; 76T soaring costs and higher prices; 79 inflation accelerating and price index soaring; 83 higher interest rates; 85 6½ prescriptions each!

Too Complex or Difficult 1 too complex; 4/2 encased in thick shielding; 15/3 chicken and egg syndrome; 28 great difficulty in holding tiny tacks; 28 virtually impossible; 40/1 difficult to get bend right; 41/1 almost impossible; 41/1 awkward; 56Ab move too drastic; 93 added complications

Deficiency or Lack 6D little or no instruction; 7 omission; 15/2 lack of recognition; 15/2 not attracted in sufficient volume; 16/1 level dangerously low; 26 not cnough orders; 33/1 depleting chromium carbide; 34/1 ill-

equipped to cope; 35/1 lagging support; 36/2 lack of confidence and continuity*; 52/2 lack of showmanship; 52/2 few notice boards

Reduction or Loss 3/2 loss of tensile strength; 4/1 loss of pressure; 56Ab staff loss; 57/2 loss of tax revenue; 73/2 flux deterioration; 104 lose heat

Unusual or Different 23/6 'freak' period; 37 false teeth don't fluoresce; 38 late publication*; 39/2 erratic operation; 57/2 out of line with world prices; 105/2 disorder

Attack or Harm Being Done 1 sued; 8 grabbed spare flesh; 11/5 and 11/6 rare birds being eaten; 12/1 vasectomy; 12/2 destroy crops; 12/2 damage drainage; 12/3 sterilised; 14/1 carpet flapping on to wet paint; 14/1 crease; 26 being laid off; 29/2 damage to it; 29/3 chipped off bits; 29/3 stones removed; 39/1 variations adversely affecting; 42/1 harm hair; 49 turpentine can damage organs in body; 50 polystyrene can cause cancer; 78 successfully sued; 84 fraud; 91/3 put out to grass; 94/2 hard on hair; 101T war; 101/2 attacks crops; 102/2 attacks flowers

Break or Failure 4/1 failed; 33 corrosion; 33 cracking; 33/1 failure; 41/3 power failure

Prevention or Restriction 10/1 restricted; 45/2 sue only after legal separation and only on property matters; 90 restrictive trade practices; 90/3 prevent or impede firms entering the market

Injury, Illness, etc. 1 injure; 5 tired; 5 teething; 8 spare tyre; 23/1 unwanted pregnancy*; 25 deaths among elderly; 32 alcoholism; 32/3 road deaths; 51 killed; 62 stretch marks; 95/1 cold, aching numbed feet; 95/2 suffering and feet swelling; 100/3 stomach upsets and vomiting; 104 hypothermic; 105 Reynaud's attack

Poor Situation   **1/1** out of date; **5** up all night; **18/1** smelly; **20** dirty*; **24** stain; **42/4** old-fashioned; **52/2** grey, dingy, disorganised, hotch-potch; **55** spray dangerously thrown up; **57/1** oil market disorganised*; **59/1** accidental ignition; **68** dampness; **83/3** creaking at the seams; **87/1** fuse blowing

Inequality/Unfairness   **45/1** take away unique status*; **45/1** wife could keep her pay cheques for herself; **45/3** damages not treated equally*

Psychological Problems   **1** discourage; **7** embarrassment; **11/1** ratty; **12/1** shock; **15/2** fail to acknowledge existence; **27** alone; **34/2** depression; **35/1** concern; **49** noticed poor recommendation; **62/3** feeling guilty or damaged; **80** depressing; **83** fears; **97** damaging to vanity

Need To Know   **58a** think of a meal; **58b** weather data; **58c** correct time; **58d** road conditions; **63** the kepi; **64/1** baffled; **65/1** which bell is ringing; **67/1** more information; **68** advice to avoid dampness; **75/3** not to be public knowledge; **77/1** public's right to know; **91/4** out of touch with advances; **98** comments; **99** opinions; **100** pill's effects; **101** effects of fungus; **102** cable characteristics; **103** how well CADC works; **106** how well Hazfile works

Unawareness   **16/2** lack of knowledge; **34/2** fail to notice; **56Ab** customer confusion; **91/4** fail to realise

Aim/Need/Requirement   **15/1** sufficient autonomy; **15/1** recognition; **21** make them think they're getting the real thing; **22** all clothes labelled; **23/3** preg-

nancy; **27** meet new friends; **29/4** new laws demanded; **41/3** accurate positioning*; **42/1** fancy a change; **42/2** desiring a more dramatic crowning glory; **46/1** need for improved fire resistance; **57/1** restore order; **59/1** a new draft; **60/2** increase overdraft; **60/2** acquire a profitable business; **61/1** floor covering; **66/1** floor for heavy pedestrian traffic; **67** new laws; **68** built-in fan; **80/2** modify negative policies and stimulate innovation; **96** move a heavy electric cooker; **102** increased power needs

Maintaining the Status Quo   **9/2** retain growth; **15/1** retain link

Impossibility   **47/2** not possible to polish or grind; **95/1** nothing could assuage . . . burden

Something Not Done or Not Available   **10/1** unavailability; **19/1** now available*; **48** now available*; **54** no choice of speeds*; **92** now available*

Decision/Dilemma   **56/1** to move or not to move; **57** to increase or not to increase; **78** judge's view; **84** Fisher dilemma

Waste of Time   **31/1** waiting list; **39/1** downtime; **41/1** time-consuming

Unpleasant Things   **18/3** germs; **53** draughts; **71/3** pest; **100/3** poisonous; **101/1** pests

Non-Agreement   **34/3** astonished when confronted with idea; **77** disagree; **84/2** dissent

Solution Failed   **11** overrun by cats; **12/3** trapping has failed; **15/3** lack of success

Penalty/Fine   **83/2** penalty

Index C: Words of Coherence

Although the aim of this book is not to investigate how clauses and sentences cohere together, the examples provide a means for initial study of that subject. This index will help you to get started, and you can compile your own indexes for other related features of language that interest you.

also 3/2, 8(2), 9/1, 22, 31/5, 33/1, 34/3, 53/2, 61/2, 73/1, 88/3, 92, 94/2, 100/3, 103/3, 103/5

as well as 82/2, 99/2

but 3/1, 9/2, 11/4, 11/5, 15/1, 15/3, 15/4, 18/5, 18/6, 18/8, 20, 23/2, 29/2, 30/1, 31/4, 33/2, 42/4, 45/3, 47/2, 54, 57/2, 62/1, 63, 71/2, 74, 77/1, 77/2, 79/2, 80/2, 82/4, 84/2, 86, 90/5, 91/2, 91/5, 92(2), 94/3, 95/1, 99/3, 100/4, 101/2, 101/4, 104(2)

cleft sentence – all 23/6, 87/2

cleft sentence – it 9/3

cleft sentence – the least 94/4

cleft sentence – what 29/2, 75/2, 91/4

compare 57/2, 73/2, 81

comparatives (including as . . . as) 10/1(2), 10/3, 15/5, 23/1, 57/2, 62/2, 62/3, 67T, 73/2, 74, 75/1, 75/2, 76T, 76/2, 77/2, 81, 82/5, 83/1, 87/1(2), 88/1, 88/3(2), 88/4(3), 96T, 103/1, 103/3

contrast 102/1

either . . . or 9/5(2), 14/1, 71/2, 86

however 7, 10/1, 33/1, 44, 45/1, 75/3, 88/3, 90/5, 93, 95/2, 100/3

in addition 3/2, 41/3, 73/2, 90/5

it (anticipatory) 9/1, 15/2, 33/1(2), 33/2, 40/1(2), 47/2, 52/1, 56/2(2), 57/1, 63, 75/3, 78, 80/3, 81, 82/4, 84/2, 92, 98/2(2), 98/4, 100/4, 102/1, 104

nevertheless 42/2

not only . . . but 8, 9/4, 53/2

only 4/2, 4/3, 15/3, 29/1, 34/2, 45/2(2), 61/2, 81, 82/4, 83/3, 84/2, 88/3, 90/6, 91/1, 97, 101/2

questions 1, 7, 23/1, 23/2, 23/3, 23/4, 58a, 58b(2), 58c(2), 58d, 60T, 60/2(2), 60/3, 63, 65/1, 65/2, 82/1, 82/5(2)

such (all types) 9/3, 11/4, 15/3, 15/5, 36/3, 43, 44, 45/1, 51, 75/2, 90/6, 91/4

superlatives 32/3, 43, 69, 75/1, 91/1, 94/5, 95/1, 101/1, 103/2

that/those (followed by specifics, e.g. *that which*) 10/1, 37, 51, 65/4, 90/5, 95/2, 99/2, 101/3

there (existential) 8, 11/6, 13/4, 15/1, 18/6, 23/1, 42/4, 48, 52/2, 57/1, 62/2, 75/3, 76/2, 77/2(2), 81, 89(3), 90/2, 90/5, 95/1, 95/2, 100/2

this/that/these/those (with following noun) 2, 3, 4/1, 4/3, 6A(2), 7(4), 8, 10/1, 10/2, 10/3, 15/3, 15/7, 23/2, 25, 28, 33/1, 34/1, 35/2, 35/3, 38(2), 46/2, 49, 50/1, 52/2, 53/2, 59/2, 61/3, 63, 65/2, 65/5, 73/1, 75/1, 75/2, 75/3(2), 87/1, 90/3, 91/2, 91/3, 93, 100/4, 102/1(2), 102/2(2)

this/that/these/those (with no following noun) 4/1, 4/3, 6C, 6D, 7, 8, 14/2, 14/3, 15/3, 15/5, 16/1, 35/3, 36/2, 42/4, 45/1, 52/1, 53/2, 56/1, 57/2, 60/3, 78, 80/2, 85/2, 86, 90/1, 93, 96(2)

which 2, 3/1(2), 4/1, 4/3(3), 9/3, 9/4, 10/1, 10/2, 11/5, 13/2, 17/2, 18/1, 30/3, 35/1, 37, 41/2, 43, 47/3, 48, 49, 50/1, 54, 61/3, 61/4, 64/1, 65/1, 65/3, 67/1, 68, 76/1(2), 82/2, 82/3, 82/5, 84/2, 84/3, 90/6, 93, 98/4, 100/2, 102/1, 102/2, 103/2

Index D: Signals of Logic

If we regard the concept of logic quite broadly as dealing with instances of cause/effect, basis/assessment and stimulus/response, we can find a large number of signals of logic in the examples, especially as problem/solution is clearly stimulus/response. No attempt is made here to index all instances of logic in the examples, but the following list of overt logic signals provides the basis for an introductory study. In addition to the words listed below, you should also examine the logic subordinators listed in Index E.

accordingly   90/5
as a result   33/1, 73/2
backed by   71/1
by . . . ing   23/1, 40/2, 49, 57/1
cause   7, 15/2, 33/1, 33/2, 39/1, 62/1, 87/1, 93, 95/2, 104(2), 105/2
dictated   46/1
effects   61/2, 90/4, 100/2
hence   33/2
in turn   10/1
lead to   6C, 78
logical   15/6
(by) means of   3/1, 3/2

mean(s)   10/1, 47/3, 76/2, 90/5, 103/4
reason   76/2
result(s)   15/7, 33/1, 59/4, 71/2, 72, 88/1, 95/1, 101/4(2), 105/2
showed   50/1
so   4/3, 12/3, 13/4, 13/5, 23/1, 25, 50/2, 60/3, 75/2, 82/1, 82/5, 97, 101/3
stemming from   102/1
thereby   33/1
therefore   4/1, 10/2, 15/6, 44, 88/3, 91/4
thus   80/1, 105/6
yet   6D, 16/1

Index E: Subordinators

apart from   9/1, 42/1
although   40/1, 87/1, 90/2, 104
as   15/5, 70, 95/2
because   1, 4/2, 11/2, 47/2, 50/1, 78, 83/3, 99/3, 101/2
despite   57/2, 85/2
due to   10/1, 88/4, 105/2
if   10/1, 11/1, 14/1, 15/2, 22, 23/3, 32/2, 41/1, 42/4, 52/1, 52/2, 76/2, 84/2
(in order) to   1, 6A, 15/3, 16/2, 36/2, 39/2(2), 46/2,

in spite of   6D, 16/1, 93
provided   23/5
since   77/2
though   79, 100/3
unless   75/1, 82/5
whatever   42/1, 57/2, 60/3
whereas   44
whether   16/1, 95/1
while (logic)   37, 63

See also time subordinators in Index H.

Index F: Hypotheticals

Whenever a writer needs to indicate doubt or uncertainty he uses a signal of hypotheticality to indicate this. Here are examples of such signalling words in the examples.

according to   88/3
apparently   33/1
appears   33/1, 71/2, 78
arguably   57/2
believes   77/2, 78, 84/2, 102/1
claimed   3/1, 30/1, 55, 71/1, 73/1, 76/2, 100/1
considered   102/1
could   57/2, 95/2, 102/1, 103/1, 103/4
estimated   102/1
evidently   74
expected   102/1
forecast   76/1
imagine   105/4
likely   75/1
look   5
may   56Ab(2), 56/2, 77/1, 77/2, 89, 90/5, 100/3, 104

might   1, 34/3
old wives' tale   62/2
perhaps   74
potential   77/2, 100/4, 103/1
probably   42/1, 80/1
promises to be   99/3, 102/1
reported   97
says   47/2, 51, 92, 100/2
seems   8, 14/1, 15/6, 49, 65/2, 74
should   6C, 23/3, 75/2
signs   76/2
so-called   71/1, 83/2, 90/3
speculation   57/1
suggests   90/4
thought   18/3, 21

Index G: Prefixes and Suffixes

Many prefixes signal problem, especially *dis*, *im*, *in* and *un*, although *re* can indicate a solution. Suffixes can indicate a problem (*ism*), a solution (*icide*), or a good evaluation (*free* and *less*). Suffixes and prefixes are thus important indicators of the structure of a text, and this index enables you to study them in context.

Prefixes

ab   **78, 90/6**
anti   **32/1, 90/3, 90/6**
contra   **23/6**
dis   **1/1, 52/2, 73/1, 77/1, 101/4, 105/2**
ill   **34/1, 67/2**
im   **28, 40/1, 41/1**
in   **30/1, 52/1, 90/2, 90/5(2)**
non   **42/4, 61/2, 61/3, 82/5**
over   **11/2(2)**
post   **34/2**
pre   **34/2**

re   **44T, 44, 52/2, 55, 71/1, 90/4(2), 91/2**
un   **10/1, 23/6(2), 42/2, 44, 57/2, 71/1, 74(2), 87/2, 90/3, 91/4, 91/5, 96, 100/3, 101/2, 101/4, 104**

Suffixes

free   **9/1, 11/3, 61/3, 62/1, 71/3**
icide   **71/3, 101/2**
ism   **32/1, 32/2, 32/3**
less   **62/2**

Index H: Time Indicators

Overt indicators of time are often important signals of the structure of the text, and this index enables you to study the effects of such words. No attempt has been made to index signals of time by tense, but tense must be considered whenever time is being studied.

after 4/4, 23/4, 45/2, 49, 53/1, 88/1, 105/1
already 5, 67/2
always 14/1, 14/3, 65/2
at last 101/1
before 4/1, 4/3, 11/5, 14/3, 41/3, 57/2
currently 102/2, 103/4, 103/6
during 23/1, 23/3, 35/2, 40/1, 62/2, 68, 73/1, 95/2
eventually 15/5
every time 8
existing 15/7, 43, 46/2(2), 73/1, 88/1, 98/2, 106/2
finally 97
first 19, 20
fresh 15T
future 43, 46/2, 91T, 91/1, 98/2, 102/1
initially 3/2, 106/3
in the past 41/1, 45/3, 86
just 47/1
later 16/4
latest 95/1
long 77/2
new 3/1, 10/2, 10/3, 15/2, 15/3, 15/4, 15/6(2), 15/7, 27, 29/4, 34/1, 45T, 45/1, 45/2, 47T, 47/2, 51, 55, 56/1, 56/2, 59/1, 67T, 67/1, 67/2(2), 73T, 73/1, 73/2, 81, 84/1, 87/1, 88/1, 88/3, 90/6, 98/2, 99/1, 99/3, 100/1(2), 102/2(2)
next 32/2
now 5, 8, 10/1, 11/6, 12/3, 13/5, 14/2, 17/4, 19, 29/4, 30/1, 33/1, 37, 42/1, 45/1, 47/2, 48/1, 56/2, 57/1(2), 70, 82/3, 88/1, 92, 95/1, 96, 101/4
old 1, 45/1, 45/2
originally 11/2
present 77/2, 83/3, 90/6
previous(ly) 45/1(2), 47/2, 88/2
prior to 23/1
recent(ly) 32/2, 52/1, 53/1, 63, 76/1, 91/1, 100/3
still 11/6, 33/2, 79/2, 80/2, 82/3, 83/3, 90/4
then 13/4, 14/2, 20, 31/3
thereafter 15/7
until 8, 10/1, 11/3, 14/2, 23/1, 28, 36/1, 49, 95/1
when 11/3, 14/1, 21, 23/3, 23/4, 34/3, 40/1, 56Ab, 64/1, 77/2, 78, 83/3, 91/1, 94/4, 101/2, 101/3, 105/6
while 31/2, 51, 61/3, 79/1, 92
yet 62/3

Index I: Informal Style Indications

Here are some indications which, in the context of their examples, contribute to informality in the style of the writing. Note that question marks, dashes and other aspects of punctuation may not always indicate some informality – it often depends on how they are used.

'And' or 'But' to Start a Sentence   11/4, 11/5, 18/8, 29, 47/2, 57, 76/2, 79/2, 85/3, 95/2, 101/4

Contractions   5, 11/1, 11/2, 21, 23, 29/2, 37, 60/3, 82, 83/1, 94/3, 97

Dashes   11/6, 13/3, 13/5, 23/6, 31/2, 32/2, 40, 42/4, 53/1, 60/3, 67/2

Exclamation Marks   15/3, 27, 53/1, 85T

Headings   11, 23, 58, 94

Imperative   58, 60/3, 95/1

Incomplete Sentences   23, 26, 27, 97

Made-Up Words   1 judge-made, 11/3 rat-free, 12 sex-mad

Particles with Verbs   24 rub away, 29/3 chipped off, 31/2 cut down

Personal Pronouns (I, You, etc.)   7, 14, 23/3, 23/4, 28, 40, 42, 52, 53, 60, 63, 68, 70, 82, 86, 94, 96

Puns   8T, 9T, 11T, 11/1 ratty, 11/5 easy meat, 14T, 18T, 31T, 49T, 64T

Questions   1T, 23, 58, 60T, 60/4, 65/1, 65/2, 81T, 82/1, 82/5

Quoted Speech   34, 67/1, 77/1, 99/3

Short Paragraphs   9, 11, 12, 13, 18, 29, 31, 32, 34, 36, 64, 65, 71, 82, 83, 85, 94, 103, 105, 106

Short Sentences   12/3, 18/8, 24, 26, 27, 60/3, 64

Suspension Points   53/2

Word Choice and Colloquialisms   8 gain a spare tyre, 8 grabbed, 8 with a bump, 11/5 went for, 13/6 get through, 21 pop, 31/2 mates, 32/1 booze, 50 dissolved before his eyes, 52/2 hotch-potch, 56Ab right under their noses, 62/2 old wives' tale, 80/2 consigned to the compost heap, 82/1 okay, 86 man enough, 91/3 put out to grass, 101T bio-war

Words in Quotation Marks   23/6, 31/3, 32/2, 39, 45/1

Index J: Key Words

Symbols

E   = evaluation
P   = problem (bad evaluation)
S   = solution or associated with solution
GE   = good evaluation (no problem)
PGE = problem or good evaluation depending on the context: *absence* of intelligence
       is a problem but *absence* of disease is a good evaluation
A   = attribute or feature of detail about something; many attributes are the basis
       for evaluations, problems and solutions:

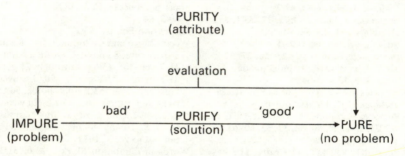

Notes

Although the classifications given will usually apply in most contexts, there could be
exceptions (e.g. being *alone* could be a solution to a personal need) and there are a few
debatable classifications (e.g. the need to *conform* could be a problem). The classifications should therefore be seen as the possible basis for study of the words in context.

A single-word entry is given for all variants (e.g. *acceptability* is the base word and
references could be to *accept, accepting, acceptability, unacceptable, acceptably*, etc.).

A	ability **15/1, 16/3, 74, 75/2, 84/3, 91/1, 95/1, 105/6**		GE	advantage **3/2, 9/1, 30/2, 73/2, 103/3**
S	abolish **98/3**		P	adverse **39/1, 100/2**
PGE	absence **88/4**		PGE	affect **16/1, 23/6, 39/1, 45/1, 62/2(2), 74**
P	abuse **78, 90/6**			
A	acceptability **9/1, 14/3, 77/2, 78, 84/1, 93, 102/1**		P	afraid **60/3**
			PGE	against **33/1, 33/2, 43, 63, 77/2**
P	accident **59/1, 99/1**		S	agreement **45/1, 77/1, 90/2, 90/4, 90/5**
A	accuracy **23/5, 41/3, 75/2**			
P	ache **95/1**		S	aimed at **67T**
S	achieve **15/1, 42/4, 61/3, 88/3, 90/4, 95/2**		P	alcoholism **32/1, 32/2, 32/3**
			P	allergy **42/1**
S	acquire **60/2**		PGE	allow **7, 9/4, 10/1, 31/5, 41/3(2), 45/2(2), 66/1, 73/1, 77/2(2), 79/1, 82/4**
S	adapt **74**			
A	adequacy **30/1, 61/4, 63**			
S	adopt **15/6**		P	alone **27, 86T**
S	advancement **15/2, 102/1**		S	answer **53/1, 84/2, 91/5**

P   anxiety   23/2
S   appeal to   15/4
A   appearance   9/4, 93
S   approach   15T
S   approval   45/1
E   argument (point of view)   77/2, 84/2
E   assessment   90/4(2)
S   assistance   22, 88/1
S   assuage   95/1
S   assure   82/5
P   astray   23/6
PGE attack   61/3, 101/2(2), 101/3(2), 105/1, 105/2(2), 105/6
S   attempt   15/3, 32/1, 57/1, 90/6, 91/1
A   attractiveness   9/4, 15/2, 15/5, 53/2, 87/2
P   attrition   15/2
A   availability   2, 4/3, 9/5, 10/1, 17/2, 17/4, 19, 42/4, 48, 71/3, 73/2, 75/3, 87/1, 92
S   avoid   23/1, 68, 95/1
GE   award   9/3, 45/3(3), 52/2
P   awkward   41/1
P   bad/worse/worst   23/6, 62/3, 82/5
P   baffled   64/1
PGE beat   31/1
GE   beauty   92, 94/1, 94/2, 94/5
GE   benefit   6A, 65/5, 79/1, 88/4
S   bid (attempt)   12/1
A   big   3/2
P   blame   76/1
GE   blessing   16/1
P   blow (shock)   12T
S   boost   18/3
P   boring   42/2
P   bother   45/1
S   break up   33/2
PGE bring down to earth   8
S   build   36/2, 91/2, 103/1, 103/2
P   bump   8
P   bunion   95/1
P   burden   95/1
PGE burgeoning   102/1
P   cancer   42/1, 50/2
P   catastrophe   11T
PGE change   1T, 1, 23/1, 34/3, 39/1, 42/1, 54, 73/2, 93, 98/2, 105/3
A   characteristics   4/3, 46/2, 61/2, 73/2
P   charges (legal)   89
PGE cheap   53/2, 83/3
P   chicken and egg syndrome   15/3
E   choice   54

A   circumference   4/3
A   cleanliness   39/1, 39/2, 61/2, 88/3, 39T, 39/2
PGE cold   95/1, 95/2, 105/2
P   collapse   40/1
PGE combat   32/1
A   compatibility   92
S   completion   4/3, 4/4, 14/3, 48, 61/1, 98/2, 106/2
PGE complex   1, 3/1, 3/2, 10/2, 56/1
P   complication   93
A   compressibility   30/2
E   compute   75/2
P   concern   35/1
E   conclusion   72, 100/4
A   condition (health)   62/3(2)
GE   confidence   23/4, 36/2
S   confirm   101/4
S   conform   61/2, 95/1
P   confusion   56Ab
E   consideration (thought)   73/1
P   consign to the compost heap   80/2
A   consistency   88/4
PGE constrain   57/2
E   consult   98/3, 99/1, 99/3
PGE contribution (adding to)   57/2, 90/4(2)
PGE control   17/3(2), 19, 23/5, 39/1, 39/2, 73/1, 88/3, 90/3, 90/6, 95/2, 101/2
A   convenience   88/3
A   conventionality   30/1, 39/1, 61/4, 73/2, 102/1, 103/1, 103/3
S   convert   91/2
S   cope   34/1, 61/4
P   corn (on foot)   95/1
A   correctness   7, 14/3, 23/3, 58c
P   corrosion   3/1, 33T, 33/1(4), 33/2(2), 43(2), 50/1, 61/2, 61/3
A   cost   3/2, 13T, 13/3, 13/6, 18/7, 53/2, 56/2, 76T, 76/1, 76/2, 87/1, 88T, 97
S   counteract   15/3, 16/2, 59/1
P   cracking   33/1(2), 33/2
P   cramped   95/2
P   creaking at the seams   83/3
P   crease   14/1
P   crisis   50T
P   criticism   90/2, 90/5
P   crowded   2
S   cure (heal)   62/3
S   cure (set)   3/2, 4/3
P   curse   16/1
PGE cut (reduce)   12/1, 13/6, 31/2, 36/1, 74

P	damage	12/2, 29/2, 49, 62/3, 78/1(2), 97, 101/2
PGE	damages (legal)	45/3(3)
P	dampness	68
P	danger	16/1, 51T, 55, 77/2, 96
PGE	death	15/2, 25, 32/2, 104
E	debate	35/2
E	decision	4/2, 53/1, 56Ab, 56/1, 65/1, 75/1, 88/1, 89
PGE	decline	15/2
S	defence	78
P	delay	38
GE	delighted	97
P	demand	29/4, 43, 66/1, 83/3
A	density	10/3, 44
P	depletion	33/1(2)
P	depression	34T, 34/2(2), 34/3, 57/1, 62/1, 62/3, 80/1
A	desirability	42/2, 42/4, 90/5
PGE	destroy	12/2
PGE	deter	90/5
P	deterioration	73/2
S	develop	3/1, 46/2
P	difficulty	6A, 28, 40/1, 65/2, 76/2, 77/2
P	dilemma	57/2, 84T, 84/2
P	dingy (dirty)	52/2
P	disappointed	57/1
P	disaster	14T
P	discourage	1
P	disease	101/3, 105/2
P	dismal	57/1
P	dissent	84/2
GE	does wonders	9/2
P	doldrums	79/2
P	downtime	39/1
PGE	drastic	56Ab
P	draught	53T, 53/1(2), 53/2
P	drawback	95/2, 97
P	dull	42/2
A	durability	88/4
P	dust	61/3
PGE	easiness	11/5, 34/2, 61/2, 81, 82/3, 84/2, 87/1, 88/3, 96T, 96
GE	economic	3/2, 58a
A	effectiveness	4/3, 17/1, 23/5, 67/1, 90/2, 90/3, 90/4(2), 100/1, 100/2, 101/1, 101/2
A	efficiency	10T, 10/1(2), 13/1, 53/2, 73/2, 90/4(2)
S	effort	36/2
S	eliminate	39/2, 87/2, 98/2
P	embarrassment	7
PGE	enable	3/1, 75/2
S	encourage	7, 34/3
PGE	end	90/4
PGE	enforce	90/5
S	enhance	9/4, 73/1
GE	enjoyment	49
S	enliven	52/2
GE	enough	9/3, 26, 40/1, 74, 83/3, 84/3, 86, 91/3
S	ensure	22, 32/2
S	eradicate	101/1
P	erratic	39/1
PGE	essential	88/4
S	establish	4/1, 15/4, 15/7
E	evaluations	70(2), 102/2, 103/4
E	examine	90/6
GE	excellent	3/1, 30/2, 69
PGE	exclude	53T, 53/1, 53/2
S	expand	54, 56/1
P	expensive	56/2
S	extend	47/2
S	extinguish	46/2
S	facelift	52/2
S	facilitate	71/2, 99/1
P	failure	4/1, 12/3, 15/3, 16/3, 33/1, 34/2, 41/3, 57/1, 59/2, 91/4
P	fall out with	64/3
P	fancy (want)	42/1, 95/1
PGE	fast	71/2
GE	favour(s)	77/2, 101/3
P	fear	1, 83/1
E	feel (think)	84/3
A	fitness	8, 91/4
A	flexibility	90/2, 90/5(2), 103/1
P	fluctuations	75/2
A	formability	3/1(2)
P	fraud	84T, 84/2(3), 84/3
P	freak	23/6
GE	free (from anxiety)	23/2
P	frigidity	74
A	fuel consumption	10/1(2)
PGE	gain	8, 15/1, 15/3, 91/3
P	gap	53/1, 63
A	gauge (size)	3/2
GE	gentle	94/4, 94/5(2)
P	germs	18/3
P	gloom	83T
P	goal (aim)	80/2
GE	good/better/best	23/5, 30/2, 67T, 69, 77/2, 82/5
PGE	great	10/3, 15/5, 28
P	guilty (feeling)	62/3
P	hammer toe	95/1
GE	happy	14/2
P	hard	15/2, 82/5, 94/2, 101/2
P	harm	42/1, 42/4, 62/2, 104
P	hazard	67/2, 96, 106/3

A   health 32/1, 37, 59/4, 67/1(2), 67/2, 71/3, 95/2, 98/1, 98/2(5), 98/4, 99/2, 104
PGE held down 36/1
S   help 9/3, 13/1, 18/3, 34/2, 34/3, 37, 56Ab, 58c, 60T, 60/3, 65/4, 75/2, 79/1, 84/1, 86, 89, 92, 93, 103T
PGE high 10/1, 30/2, 32/3, 33/1, 43, 53/2, 59/2, 73/2, 76T, 76/2, 83/1, 90/4, 91/1, 102/1(2), 102/2(2)
P   hotch-potch 52/2
A   hygiene 61/2
P   hypothermic 104
GE   ideal 10/1
P   ignore 11/5
P   illness 23/6
P   impaired 65/5
P   impede 90/3
S   implementation 15/7(2), 99/3
PGE important 9/1, 9/4, 58c, 75/1, 100/4, 104
S   improvement 6C, 9/4, 10/1, 42/3, 43T, 46/1, 52T, 52/1, 67/2, 71/2, 73T, 73/1, 90/4, 102T, 102/1
PGE increase 10/1(2), 25, 42/1, 46/1, 52/1, 60/2(2), 71/2(2), 73/2, 76/1, 76/2
GE   in favour of 77/2
P   infection 71/2, 101/3
P   inhibit 80/2
S   initiate 73/1
P   injury 1
E   inspect 4/2
S   institute (start) 35/2
A   intelligence 56Ab, 74
P   interfere 23/5
P   intervene 75/2
E   investigate 4/2, 100/1, 102/1, 102/2
S   iron out 75/2
P   issue (contention) 84/2
GE   just (legal) 84/1
E   justify 56/2
PGE keep out 44
PGE kill 25, 51, 101/3
P   lack 15/2, 15/3, 16/2, 52/2
P   lagging 35/1
P   lax 81T
PGE lay off 26
GE   leading (first) 75/1
A   length (time) 73T, 73/2, 75/3, 95/2
P   let down 37
A   life (shelf) 30/2, 73T, 73/2, 92(2)

P   little (quantifier) 6D, 7, 56Ab, 104
P   loss 3/2, 4/1, 56Ab, 57/2, 91/4, 104(3)
PGE low 10/1, 16/1, 27, 30/2, 44, 76/2, 88/4
P   mad 12T, 12/1
PGE maintain 76/2, 87/1, 88/2, 88/3, 90/4
S   make 40/2, 44, 50/1, 53/1, 78
P   maraud 12/2
S   meet (needs) 46/2, 66/1, 102/1
S   minimise 100/3
S   modify 80/2, 103/3(2)
E   monitor 105/3
PGE more/most 8, 9/1, 13/1, 15/5(4), 16/1(2), 18/6, 23/1, 56/1, 62/2, 63, 67/1, 71/2, 76/1, 82/4, 83/3, 90/3, 90/5, 101/3, 103/4
S   mount (start) 15/3
A   naturalness 15/2, 23/5(2), 42/3, 42/4(2), 82/1, 82/5
GE   neat 40/2, 53/2
A   necessity 4/1, 87/2
P   need 15/3, 46/1, 52/2, 56Ab, 60/2, 62/3, 78T, 87/2, 99/3, 102/1
P   negative 80/2
P   neglect 80/1
GE   nice 9/1
PGE no 2(2), 3/1, 6D, 10/3, 15/1, 62/2, 62/3, 64/2, 80/2(2), 82/5, 84/2, 100/2
A   normality 3/2, 23/4, 37, 71/2(2), 82/3, 90/6, 92
P   not (or n't) 5, 14/3, 15/2, 16/3, 18T, 23/5, 23/6, 26, 29/2, 30/2, 32/2, 33/2, 37, 45/3, 47/2, 49T, 49, 52/1, 60/3, 61/4, 69, 74(2), 75/3(2), 77/1, 77/2(3), 78(2), 79/1, 80/2, 82/3, 82/4, 82/5, 83/1, 83/3, 84/2, 84/3, 86, 89, 90/6, 91/5, 92, 94/3, 95/1, 98/2, 100/3
GE   notable 74
P   numb 95/1
P   objective 90/4
A   obtainability 42/4
S   offer 48
S   offset 15/2
GE   okay 82/1
PGE old-fashioned 42/4
P   omission 7(2)
S   open doors 15/2
E   opinion 99/1
S   optimise 17/3(2)

GE order (organised) 57/1, 75/1, 105/2

A organisation 16/2, 17/1, 52/2, 91/2

P out of (line, etc.) 1, 57/2, 71/2, 91/4

S overcome 9/3, 15/3, 65/2, 73/1, 86, 87/1, 96

PGE overrule 78

PGE overrun 11/2(2)

S partially 101/2

P penalty 83/2

A performance 46/2(2), 54, 71/2, 100/2

S permit (verb) 1(2), 3/2, 77/2, 92

P pest 71/3, 101/1, 101/2, 101/4

S plan 9/1, 12/1, 17/3(2), 32/2, 52/2

GE pleasant 73/1, 88/4

GE pleased 7

P poison 100/3

A porosity 10/3

A possibility 4/2, 7, 23/2, 28, 40/1, 41/1, 47/2, 52/1(2), 63

A practicality 14/3

S precaution 68

GE precise 40/2

P premature 100/4, 104

S preserve 82/4, 92(5)

A pressure 4/1(2), 4/4, 59/2

S prevent 33T, 33/1, 40/1, 62/3, 90/2, 90/3, 90/5, 105/6

A price 36T, 36/1, 53/1, 57/1, 57/2(5), 75/1, 76, 76/1, 76/2, 79/2, 90/4(2)

P problem 1, 3/2, 4/1, 4/2, 9/2, 9/3, 15/2, 30/1, 32/2, 34/2, 37, 39/2, 41/2, 56Ab, 56/2, 57T, 59/1, 60/3, 61/4, 62/1, 63/1, 65/1, 65/3, 65/4, 68, 73/1, 84/1, 86, 87/1, 89(3), 91/5, 96, 100/3

S promote (improve) 73/1

A properties (of materials) 3/1, 10/1, 67/2

S proposal 35/1, 35/2, 67/2, 77/2, 98/2(4), 98/4, 99/1, 99/3

A propriety 51

S protect 25, 29/4, 33/1, 33/2, 43T, 43(2), 51(2)

S provide 48, 54, 67/1, 73/1, 106/1, 106/3

A purity 100/3

PGE push up (increase) 76/1

PGE put out to grass 91/3

P puzzle 100T

P quicksand 34/2

PGE raise 10/1, 57/1(2), 57/2

P ratty 11/1

A recognition 15/1, 15/2(3), 15/5(2), 99/3

S recommend 35/3, 46/1, 46/2, 49, 80/2(2), 84/1, 89, 92, 104

PGE reduce 10/1, 55, 87/1, 88T, 93, 104, 105/2

P refuse 8, 84/2

E regard (view) 16/1

P regret 75/3

A regularity 23/6

S regulate 46/1, 46/2, 51, 67/2, 84/1

P reject 88/4

S rejuvenate 71/1

A relevance 46/1

A reliability 23/5, 23/6

S remedy 6A, 35/1, 67/1, 90/3

PGE remove 14/3, 84/1, 86, 90/2, 90/4

S repair 4/3, 4/4

S repel 92(2)

S replacement 10/1, 18/5, 30/3, 48, 52/2, 88/1, 88/2, 98/2

S request 2, 70, 98/2, 98/3

P requirement 4/3, 17/3, 22, 30/2, 48, 56Ab, 60/3, 61/2, 61/3, 67/2, 88/2

S reroute 55

S rescue 74

E research 3/1, 59/4, 71/1, 81

S reshape 71/1

A resilience 4/3

A resistance 3/1, 4/3, 46T, 46/1(2), 46/2, 47/1, 61/2, 61/3(2), 71/2, 93

GE resourceful 69

S response 57/1, 70

S restore 57/1, 74

P restricted 10/1, 90T, 90/1, 90/2(2), 90/4(2), 90/5, 90/6

PGE retain 9/2, 15/1

PGE retard 46/2

E review 80/2, 90/1, 98/2

S revitalise 35/3

GE right 5, 40/1, 65T, 84/3

PGE rise 23/1, 76/1(2), 76/2, 85/2, 105/3, 105/6

P risk 49, 56Ab, 95/1

PGE rough 78

S rub away 24

A safety 23/2(2), 41/3, 47/1, 81, 99/2

A saleability 18/3, 53/1, 90/4(2), 101/2

GE satisfactory 86

S saving 88/3, 104T, 104(2)

P scratch 47/1

E scrutiny 98/4

S   search   **2**
S   seek   **60/2**
E   select   **54, 103/2, 106/3**
GE sensible   **8**
A   seriousness   **34/3, 62/1, 84/2**
S   set up (start)   **4/3**
A   severity   **76/1**
P   shame   **8**
A   shape   **3/1, 9/4, 9/5, 10/2, 10/3, 71/1, 93**
S   shield   **4/2**
P   shock   **12/1**
PGE short-circuit   **13T**
P   sickness   **34/3**
A   significance   **90/5**(2), **102/1**
A   simplicity   **7, 23/3, 40/2, 65/4, 90/5, 98/2**
A   size   **4/3, 17/2, 19, 95/2**
A   slimness   **8, 82/1**
P   slip   **61/2**
PGE smash   **64/1**
P   smelly   **18/1**
A   smoothness   **41/3**
PGE soaring (increasing)   **76T, 79/2**
S   solution   **1, 15/7, 30/1, 41/1**(2), **41/2, 60/3, 61/4, 65/3**
S   soothe   **5**
P   spasm   **105/2**
PGE special   **4/2, 4/3, 10/1, 16/3, 30/2, 30/3, 51, 65/2, 73/1, 98/2, 102/2**
GE spectacular   **101/4**
A   stability   **30/2, 73/1**(2), **73/2**
P   stain   **24**(2)
PGE stem (stop)   **83/3**
PGE sterilise   **12/3**
S   stimulate   **80/2**
PGE stop   **105/1**
S   strategy   **23/3**
GE strength   **3/1, 3/2, 10/3, 30/2, 84/3, 90/5, 95/2, 97**(2), **98/2, 102/2, 104**
P   stress   **23/6, 33/1**(2), **33/2**
P   stretch marks   **62T, 62/1, 62/2**(2), **62/3**(2)
P   stringent   **61/2**
GE success   **4/3**(2), **9T, 15/3, 16/3, 52/2, 78, 101/4**(2)
PGE sue   **1, 45/2**(2), **78**
P   suffer   **34/2, 34/3, 62/3, 94/1, 95/2**
GE sufficient   **15/1, 15/2, 63**
S   suggestion   **4/3, 34/3, 90/3**
GE suitable   **4/3, 10/1, 22, 30/3, 44**(2), **47/2, 53/2, 74, 92**
GE super   **80/1**
E   support (backing)   **15/7**(2), **35/1**
PGE suppress   **73/2**

S   survival   **15T**
P   susceptible   **43, 101/3**
P   swelling   **95/2**
S   sympathy   **62/3**
S   tackle   **84/1**
PGE take away   **45/1**
P   take out/their toll   **4/1, 94/3**
P   tear   **62/2**
P   teething   **5**
E   test   **4/1**(2), **4/3**(2), **4/4, 31T, 31/1, 31/2, 59T, 59/1, 71/2, 81, 88/1, 100/2**(2), **100/4, 101/4, 102/2**(2), **103/6, 104**
E   think   **58a, 84/3, 91/1, 91/2**
A   thinness   **62/2**(2)
GE thorough   **94/5**(2)
P   time-consuming   **41/1**
P   tired   **5**
P   too   **1, 3/2, 8, 14/1, 56Ab, 56/2**(2), **81T, 90/4, 90/5, 104**
P   toxic   **49, 61/3, 67/2**
PGE trapping   **12/3**
S   treat(ment)   **62/3, 92**
P   trouble   **5, 14/1, 42/1, 62/1**
S   try   **4/3, 5, 22, 23/1, 23/3, 89**
GE understand   **1, 6A, 11/1, 16/1, 62/3, 75/3**
P   unduly   **90/2**
P   unfortunately   **23/6**
P   unsightly   **87/2**
P   upset   **23/6, 62/1, 100/3**
P   urgent   **48**
GE usable   **52/1**
S   use (noun)   **6D, 7, 10/1, 17/1, 18/5, 40/1, 61/2, 61/4, 73/2, 78, 86, 88/4, 92**
S   use (verb)   **4/1, 4/3, 13/1, 16T, 22, 23/2, 29/3, 42/3**(2), **42/4**(2), **46/1, 47/2, 51, 52/2, 53/2, 59/1, 61/3, 73/1, 86**(2), **92, 96, 103/1, 103/4, 103/6, 105/1**
GE useful   **62/3, 91/3**
A   value   **52/1, 56/2**
PGE vasectomy   **12/1**
GE victory   **79/1**
E   view (opinion)   **77/2, 78**
A   viscosity   **4/3**
A   vital   **71/2, 73/1, 94/2, 104**
P   vomiting   **100/3**
P   vulnerable   **44**
P   wait/await   **31/1, 31/2**(2), **31/3, 31/4, 91/3**
P   wander off   **96**
P   want   **68, 83/1**
P   war   **101T**

S   ward off **18/3**

P   weakness **16/1, 90/3, 104**

GE   welcome **75/1, 84/1**

GE   willing **38, 57/2**

P   wilt **101/3**

P   wish **15/1(2), 104**

S   withstand **22, 47/3, 102/1**

P   woe **15/7**

GE   wonder **71/1**

A   worth **49**

Index K: Subject Index

advertisements 2, 6, 21–2, 31, 46–7, 51, 53, 58, 78, 80, 91–2, 121–2
aims 18, 20, 33, 74, 77–9, 86
ambition 20
artefacts 38–9, 53
assessment 89, *90–6*, 101, 103–6, 113–15, 118–20, 122, 128, 129, 130, 131, 133, 134
attitudes 7
attributes 12–14, 27, 89

basis 89, *90–6*, 101–6, 113–15, 118, 119, 122, 128–30, 133
bold type 49, 122
but and *however* 10, 24, 25, 27, 30–2, 48, 57, 66, 68, 77, 84, 85, 99, 105, 111, 115, 118, 119, 121, 134, Index C

cause of problem 18, 21, 22, 33, 46, 83, 107
comparative evaluation 18, 76, 111, *114–18*, *125–35*
compound words 6, 33, 51
condensed structures 17, 18, 30, 36, *53*, 72
contractions 2, 43, 79
critical analysis *1*, 3, 6, 7

decision 20, *74–9*, 86, 99, 102, 130–2, 134
Deficiency in solution 5, 18, 30, 33, 61–6, 71, 72, 111, 114, 119–21
description 11–14, 36, 37, 40, 53, 57, 86, 91, 93
desire 20
difference 64–7, 71, 91, 106
dilemma 20, *76*, 77, 86
disagreement 25, 96, *101–4*, 107, 118
discussion papers 124, 125
doctor 21, 22, 52

editorials 98–100
ellipsis 11, 40
essay 98–9
evaluation 5, 16–27, 30, 31, 33, 37–54, 58, 62, 66, 72, 76, 78, 79, 81, 82, 84, 86, 89, *90–135*
examples xiii–xvi, 4

failure *31*, 33, 34, 77, 86
figures and units 93, 94
forecast 100, 101

function 11, 14

general specific 30
genre 2, 31, 33, 122

headings 34, 43, 44, 46, 77, 93
hypotheticals 10, 49, 68, 84, 91, 92, 100, 131, 134, Index F

impartiality *96–8*, 128
imperative 41, 44, 46, 70, 78, 123
implementation 16, 18, 21, 22, 32, 38, 52, 71, 126, *132–4*
importance 10, 12, 13, 29, 30, 36, 38, 104, 126
improvement 7, 18, 57, *61–73*, 94–5, 111, 114, 119, 126
incomplete sentences 44, 46, 77
indexes 6, 7, 13, 24
incomplete structures 36, 40
information not included 3, 8–10, 36–50, 57, 66, 92, 115, 118, *132*, 133

letters 24, 25, 47, 85
location of problem 16, 18

misunderstanding 4, 120

needs 18, 34, 74, *77*, 78, 80–2, 120
need-to-know 77, 78, *84–6*, 87, 102, 132
negation 9, 10, 45, 46, 59, 70, 90, 97, 103, 118, 120, 122, 125, 127, Index G
new product 26, 27
not only . . . but also 25, 26, Index C

opinion 2, *95*, 96, 107, 115
order (sequence) 23, 24, 29, 68

paragraphs 1, 26, 31, 39, 78, 80, 118, 119
partial structures 18
passive voice 2, 59, 60, 69, 110
pre-evaluation 27, 31, 106, *110–11*, 122, 123, 132
prejudices 7
problem – most pages, *see* Contents
'Problem–Solution' structure *44–7*, 50, 136
'Problem–Solution–Evaluation' structure 49–51
progress reports 33
pronouns 2, 25, 45, 58, 60, 84, 85, 99

proposals 48, 53, 116, 118, 125, 126
pros and cons 43, 44, 77, 86, 99, 134
psychological problems 74, *83*, 84, 86, 107
public discussion 125–6
punctuation 1, 26, 38, 39, 43, 51, 60, 61, 64, 85, 106, 121, 124
puns 31, 39, *53*

questions answered 9, 11, 12, 20, 28, 78, 79, 112

reader needs and knowledge 3, 8, 9, 17, 30, 36, 38, 40, 42, 44, 49, 50, 51, 53, 91, 98, 120, 125, 132
requirements 74, *80–2*
reviews 90, 96–8
rulings 103, 104

selection of information 13, 24, 28, 30, 104
sentence length 1, 4, 9, 60, 61, 64, 80, 97
seriousness of problem 16, 18, 50, 52, 70, 71, 83, 129
side effects 22, 127
signals of structure 3, 4, 6, 15, 18, 24, 30, 57–61
signs and notices 86
similarities 64–7, 71
situation – most pages
'Situation' structure 51, 89, *104–5*
'Situation–Evaluation' structure 41, 51, 89, 100, 104, *105–7*
'Situation–Problem–Solution' structure 37, 38, *47–8*

'Situation–Problem–Solution–Evaluation' structure 1, 5, 15, 17, 18, *21–35*, 36, 41, 89, 136
skilled opinion *95–8*, 107, 115
'Solution' structure 40
'Solution–Problem' structure *46*, 52, 66
standards 80, 81, *82*, 83, 96–8
style (formality/informality) 1, *2*, 6, 31, 32, 41–6, 48, 49, 51, 52, 58–61, 65, 67, 70, 72, 77–80, 85, 86, 90, 91, 94, 105, 122, 123, Index I
summaries *8*, 11, 12, 15, 17, 27–8, 32, 36, 39, 46, 50–4, 66, 81, 92, 118

telegrams 8, 9
tense 9
testing 16, 18, 89, *125–39*
this 16, 24, 25, 37, 70, 104, Index C
that 44, 111, Index C
time signals 11, 22, 25, 30, 32, 47, 48, 66, *67–9*, 70, 118, 120, Index H
titles 1, 14, 30, 39, 51, 52, *53*, 69, 75, 94, 115, 122, 126, 131
too 5, 53, 75, 106, Index J

unskilled opinion 98

value judgement 103, *130*, 134

warnings 41
word choice 1, 2, 42, 51, 58, 70
writer's viewpoint 4, 28, 29, 38, 39, 46, 104, 106, 119